YOU CAN DRAW

DORLING KINDERSLEY

LONDON, NEW YORK, MUNICH,
MELBOURNE, and DELHI

SENIOR DESIGNER Robert Perry
DESIGNER Jon Hall
PUBLISHING MANAGER Simon Beecroft
DTP DESIGNER Lauren Egan

PROJECT EDITOR Laura Gilbert
CATEGORY PUBLISHER Alex Allan
PRODUCTION Rochelle Talary
FRONT COVER ART Brandon Peterson

First American Edition, 2006
06 07 08 09 10 9 8 7 6 5 4 3 2 1

Published in the United States by DK Publishing, Inc.
375 Hudson Street, New York, New York 10014

Published in Great Britain by Dorling Kindersley Limited.

ISBN 0-7566-1470-8

A catalog record is available from the Library of Congress.

Color reproduction by Media Development and Printing Ltd, U.K.
Printed and bound in China by Leo Paper Products Ltd.

DK books are available at special discounts for bulk purchases for
sales promotions, premiums, fund-raising, or educational use.
For details, contact:

DK Publishing Special Markets
375 Hudson Street
New York, NY 10014
SpecialSales@dk.com

YOU CAN DRAW

MARVEL
CHARACTERS

BY DAN JURGENS

CONTENTS

INTRODUCTION

I've met many fans who have asked me, "What's the magic
secret for becoming a comic-book artist?" The truth is,
my answer is always the same.

"Draw."

While that doesn't sound too exciting, it's the truth!

Draw as much as you can. Draw your favorite characters, the
car parked in your driveway, someone snoozing in front of
the TV set, the odd-looking light on the coffee table, or your
friends as they play in the yard. Draw anything and everything
you can think of. Try it with different pencils, markers,
and pens. Draw small. Draw big.

Just draw!

I can't promise you success as a great comic artist, but if you
develop a love for drawing and a little self-discipline it will
certainly help you along the way.

Beyond that, who knows?

You might just become the next guy to draw Spider-Man
clinging to the top of the Empire State Building!

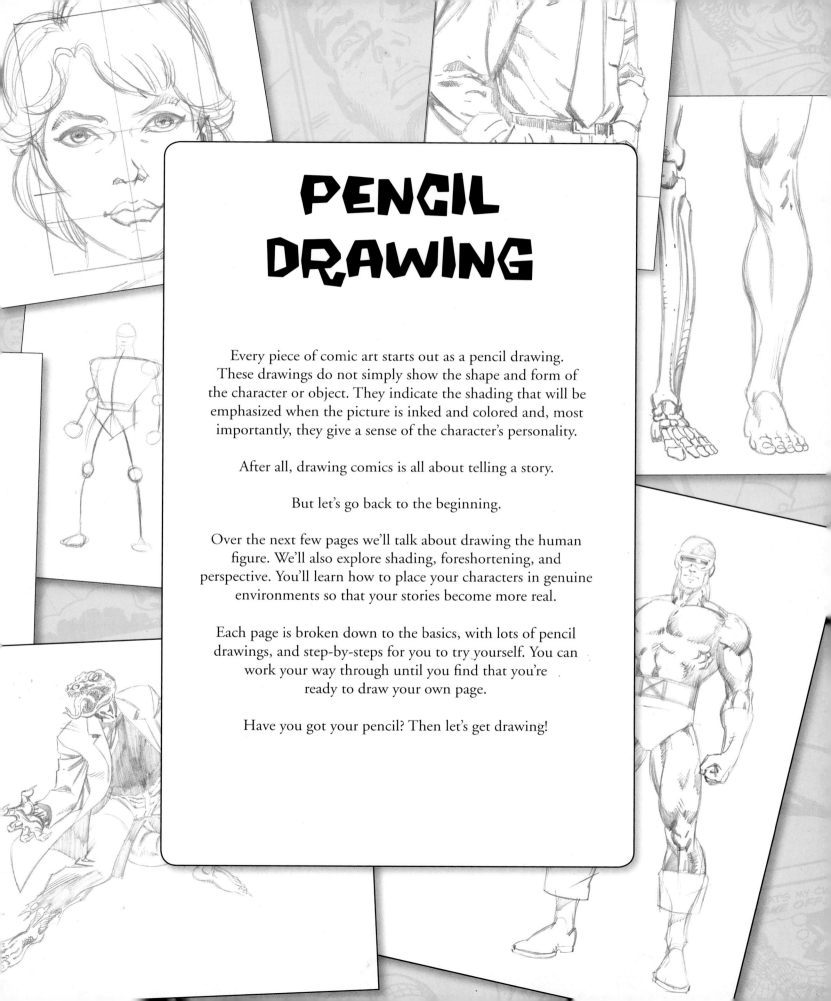

PENCIL DRAWING

Every piece of comic art starts out as a pencil drawing. These drawings do not simply show the shape and form of the character or object. They indicate the shading that will be emphasized when the picture is inked and colored and, most importantly, they give a sense of the character's personality.

After all, drawing comics is all about telling a story.

But let's go back to the beginning.

Over the next few pages we'll talk about drawing the human figure. We'll also explore shading, foreshortening, and perspective. You'll learn how to place your characters in genuine environments so that your stories become more real.

Each page is broken down to the basics, with lots of pencil drawings, and step-by-steps for you to try yourself. You can work your way through until you find that you're ready to draw your own page.

Have you got your pencil? Then let's get drawing!

EQUIPMENT

PENCILS

The most common type of pencil is a graphite one encased in wood that features a variety of leads. A popular type is a mechanical pencil that holds several thin leads. Blue pencils are used because the marks won't show in photographic reproduction.

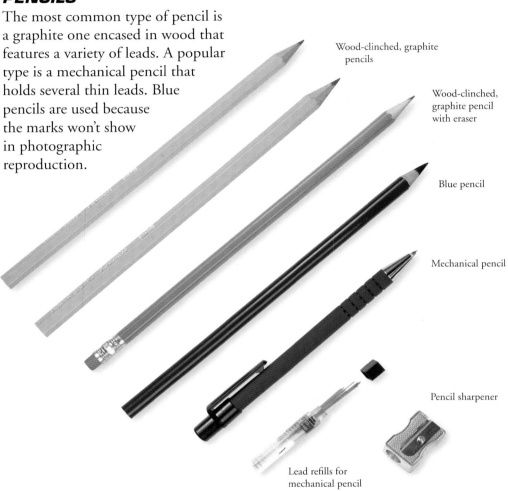

Wood-clinched, graphite pencils

Wood-clinched, graphite pencil with eraser

Blue pencil

Mechanical pencil

Pencil sharpener

Lead refills for mechanical pencil

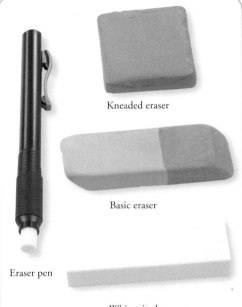

Kneaded eraser

Basic eraser

Eraser pen

White vinyl eraser

Erasers

No one draws a perfect line every time, which is why we need erasers. A basic rubber eraser does a fine job but can crumble with use. A kneaded eraser can be shaped to the specific area you want to erase and doesn't leave a mess. A white vinyl eraser is gentle and doesn't crumble. An eraser pen is good for small sections because you have more control over it.

PENCIL GRIP

Grasp the pencil—not too tightly—between the thumb and middle finger while using the index finger to "steer" or guide it. Keep your fingers and wrist loose. This enables you to have more consistently graceful, sweeping lines. Don't push down too hard or you may leave permanent impressions in the paper.

MARVEL EXPERT ADVICE

It is a good idea to try a number of different pencils and lead types before you decide on your particular favorite. Different pencils create different effects and this is true for different types of lead. Remember that a pencil that is unsuitable for the drawing that you're working on today might be perfect for the one you tackle tomorrow. Have your favorites but don't be afraid to try other types for different sorts of drawing!

PENCIL MARKS

True drawing pencils come in different grades. The letter "H" stands for "hardness." 4H and above means that the pencil has an increasingly harder lead. The letter "B" indicates "blackness." 4B and above means the lead gets steadily softer. HB is right in between.

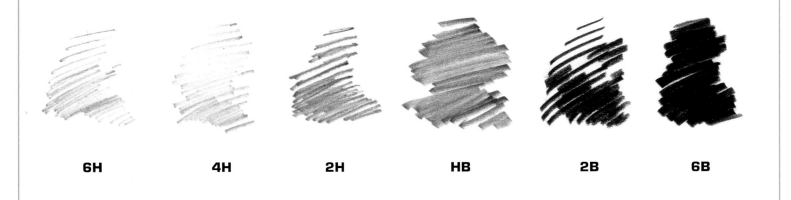

6H　　　　**4H**　　　　**2H**　　　　**HB**　　　　**2B**　　　　**6B**

Other equipment

A straight edge, like a raised ruler, is an absolute must. "Raised" means that a portion of the upper plane of the ruler doesn't touch the paper. It leaves a slight gap, which prevents smearing. A triangle or set square, compass, French curve, and assorted stencils or templates complete your toolbox.

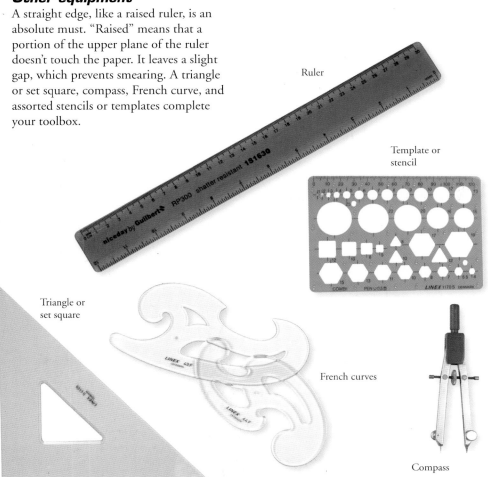

Ruler

Template or stencil

Triangle or set square

French curves

Compass

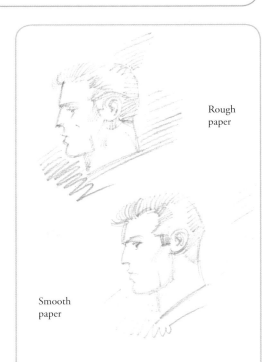

Rough paper

Smooth paper

Paper

Some artists prefer working on rough paper because they like the feeling that the pencil is gripping to the paper as they draw and the textured effect that appears in the line. Others prefer a smooth paper because the pencil moves across the page with ease and doesn't dig into the paper.

BASIC SHAPES

SHAPING UP

The basic structure of almost any object can be drawn using combinations of simple shapes. There are three main shape groups. The first includes squares, rectangles, cubes, and cuboids. The second is made up of circles, spheres, and cylinders. The third consists of triangles and pyramids.

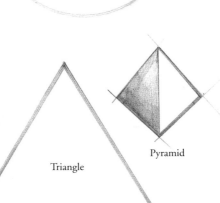

Cylinder

Sphere

Circle

SQUARES, CUBES, RECTANGLES, AND CUBOIDS

Many objects feature squares and rectangles, and their 3-D versions: cubes and cuboids. A TV set, toaster, or refrigerator can be drawn from these basic shapes.

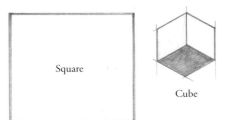

Square

Cube

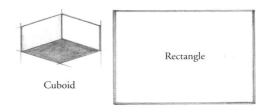

Cuboid

Rectangle

CIRCLES, SPHERES, AND CYLINDERS

Check your kitchen for circular, spherical, or cylindrical shapes. You will see these basic forms in items including drinking glasses, candles, and lightbulbs.

TRIANGLES AND PYRAMIDS

Triangle- and pyramid-shaped forms may be harder to find. Many lampshades and light fixtures are a combination of cylinders and pyramids.

Triangle

Pyramid

COMMON EXAMPLES OF SHAPES

You see many of these objects on a daily basis but you may not have thought about the basic shapes that make up their form. Look at them now and try to identify the different shapes used for each object.

Master the basics

Using different shapes together lets you create more complex drawings. A house is a cube with rectangles for the windows and door, along with a triangle on top. Several cuboids could become an office building, or even a cityscape that Spider-Man might swing through (above left). In the other picture, a cuboid with a smaller one on top forms the basic structure of the police car. A long cylinder with a circle on each end becomes Johnny Storm's motorcycle.

VEHICLES

This X-Jet is made up of shapes from all of the three basic shape groups. The wings are made of triangular shapes while the main body of the jet is a cuboid that is rounded into a cylinder.

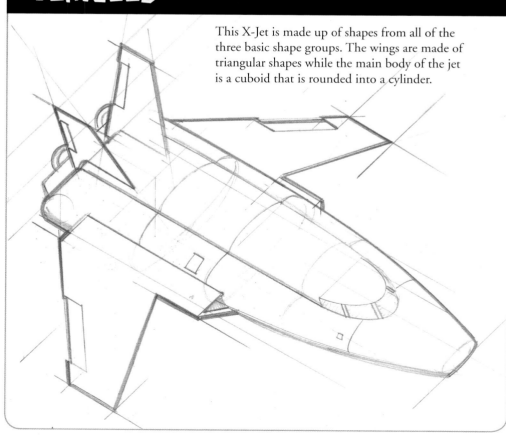

Start with something simple like a TV set, drinking glass, or lamp that represents an obvious basic shape. Begin your sketch with the simple shape and then add the detail necessary to define your object. When you have conquered that, combine shapes for more complex drawings. It's easier than you think!

THE FIGURE

BRANCHING OUT

The first human body you ever drew was probably a common stick figure. Believe it or not, it is a technique that will still work for you today. Using a simple stick figure as a basis allows you to build a solid foundation for your figure.

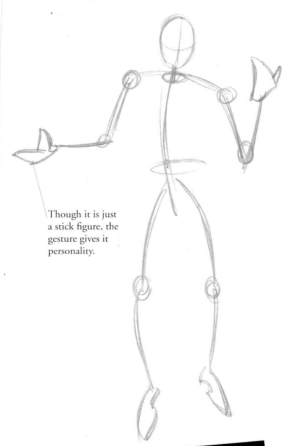

Though it is just a stick figure, the gesture gives it personality.

MARVEL EXPERT ADVICE

I always start with the head and then sketch in the spine, or central axis, of the figure in order to get the pose or action I want. After that I move on to the shoulders, arms, and legs. Once I'm satisfied with the pose, I flesh out the trunk (main part of the body), arms, and legs until the simple stick figure has become a recognizable human being!

PRACTICE MAKES PERFECT

Drawing stick figures of existing characters can help you see how useful it is to start with a basic approach. If your stick figure is correct, the chances are that your final figure drawing will be correct as well. Try drawing stick figures of these three characters, paying particular attention to the different poses.

Spider-Man
Crouching close to the ground, Spidey is ready to leap.

Elektra
With her three-pronged daggers, Elektra launches her attack.

Wolverine
Packed with muscle, this X-Men member pounds the ground as he walks.

COMPLETE FIGURE

Use these stages to work up a drawing of Cyclops. Sketch lightly at first, building the figure as you go, and making the lines gradually bolder.

1) Start with a simple oval for the head, adding light lines to show where the eyes and nose will be.

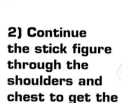

2) Continue the stick figure through the shoulders and chest to get the basic pose.

3) Add arms, with circles representing the shoulders, elbows, and hands.

4) Draw down through the legs, using circles for the knees and feet. Watch how the body is fitting together.

5) "Flesh out" Cyclops now, using three-dimensional shapes. This will give weight to his trunk, arms, and legs.

6) As you add muscle and costume detail, like Cyclops's glasses, you can erase lines that you don't need. You will learn how to add detail later, but give it a go now!

STEP-BY-STEP

MALE FIGURE

IN PROPORTION

When drawing the human figure, all the parts of the body should fit together accurately. This is called "proportion." For example, if your figure has arms longer than the legs, your drawing is "out of proportion." Using a grid, as shown on the opposite page, will help make your figure look consistent and proportionally correct.

Marvel classics

These Marvel Super Heroes are similar heights, but their physiques differ to give either a bulky or sleek appearance.

Captain America

Thor

Daredevil

EVOLUTION OF A CHARACTER

Spider-Man debuted over 40 years ago when it was common for comic-book Super Heroes to be drawn in more realistic proportions. Over the years, his size and physical stature increased. As more time passed, his poses became crazier and even more "bug-like" to emphasize the uniqueness that is pure Spidey!

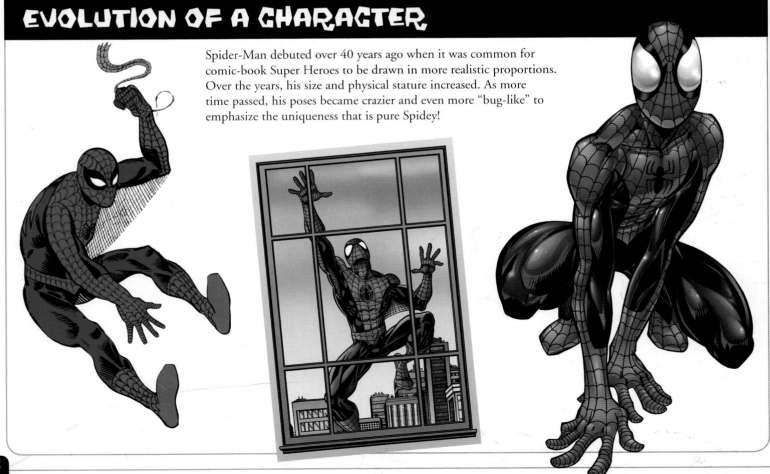

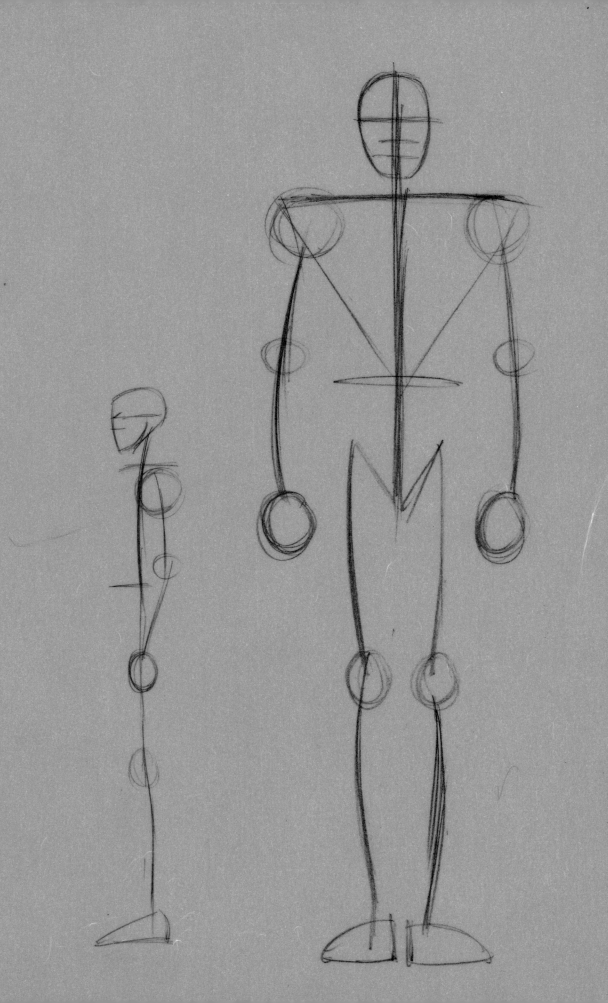

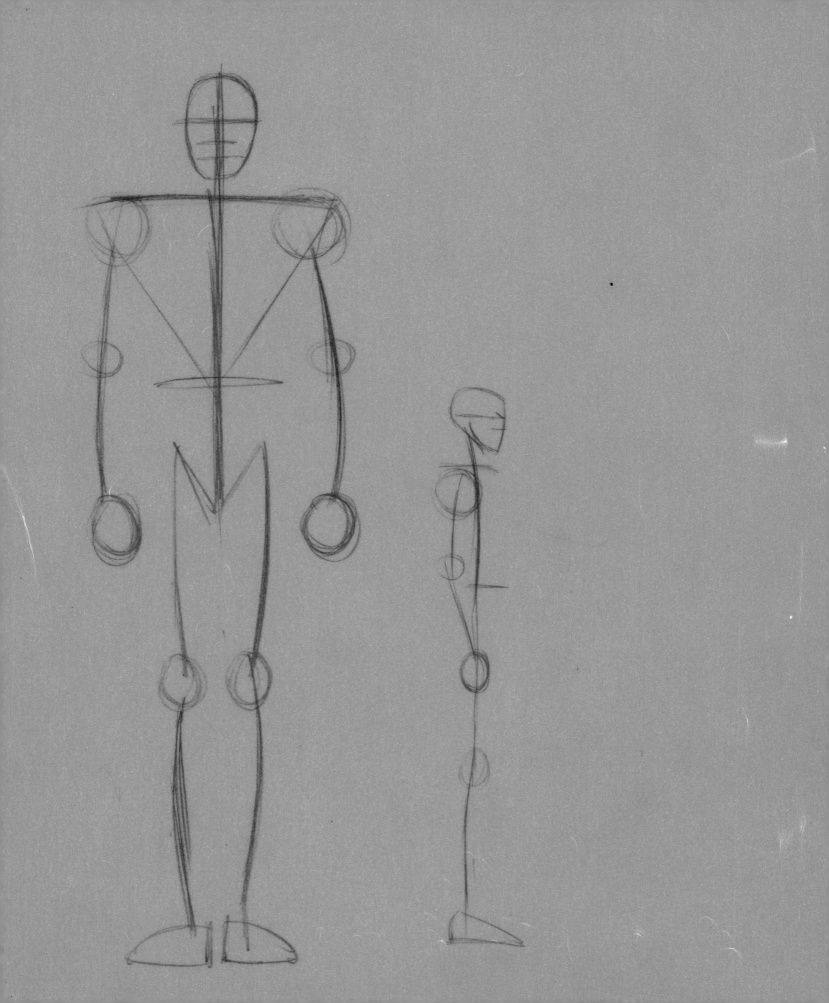

Reed Richards

Proportion also relates to the setting around the body or the objects that a character might be holding. In this illustration, Reed Richards's hand is obviously in proportion to his head and shoulders. This is also the case with the cup that he is holding. In addition, the muscles on his figure are well placed and relate to the relaxed pose that Reed is in.

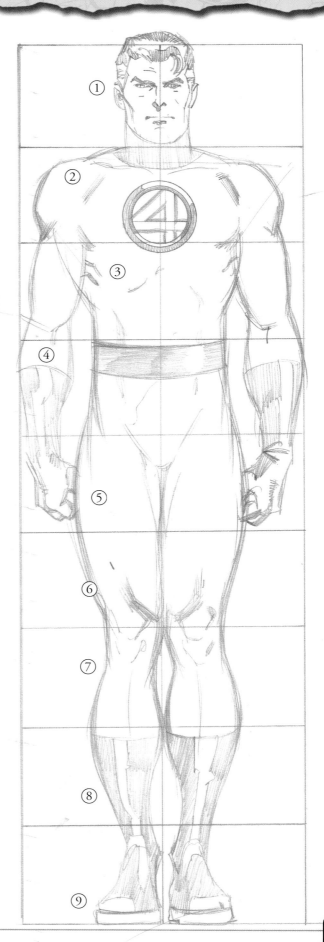

THE MEASUREMENTS

Most men are six to seven heads tall. But these are Marvel characters we're talking about, and to keep them heroic in proportion, they should be nine heads tall.

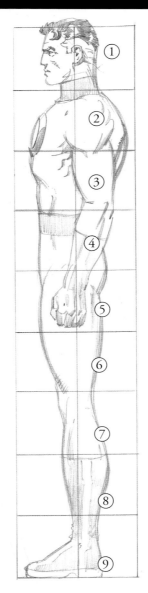

① Draw a grid that is nine boxes high with a vertical axis (line going down through the middle). Rough in an oval for the head.

② Move on to the shoulders. To be a true Marvel hero—or villain—the shoulders should be about three heads wide.

③ Work down through the trunk and arms. The biceps should end by the time you get to the bottom of this box.

④ Now the biceps develop into forearms and the body trims to a narrow waistline.

⑤ With the arms at the sides, the hands will naturally fall here as the legs widen from the torso or trunk.

⑥ The legs begin to narrow again as they reach their own center point: the knees.

⑦ Once again, the legs thicken, though not as far as before, and taper or narrow down through the calves…

⑧ … and through the lower shins…

⑨ … until we end with the ankles and feet. Take a break! You've earned it!

FEMALE FIGURE

BODYBUILDING

The basics remain the same but drawing the female figure is quite different from drawing the male figure. A female figure will taper more at the waist and widen at the hips. Her arms and legs will tend to be more slender and she will generally have smaller hands and feet. As with the male figure, remember to keep the body in proportion.

Marvel classics

These figures have similar body shapes but notice how their different costumes and hairstyles create very different effects.

Invisible Woman

Storm

Elektra

EVOLUTION OF A CHARACTER

Jean Grey, one of the original X-Men, first appeared over 40 years ago. In the beginning, she was a rather meek woman who called herself Marvel Girl. She later evolved into the incredibly powerful Phoenix and then transformed into the villainous Dark Phoenix. The different artworks reflect these personality changes.

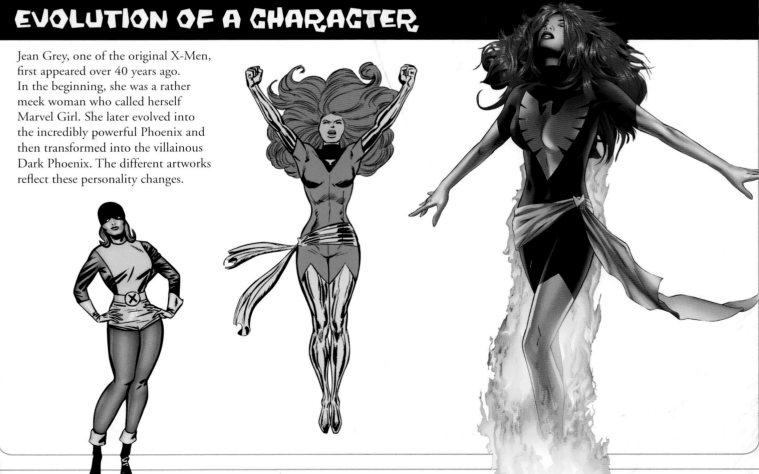

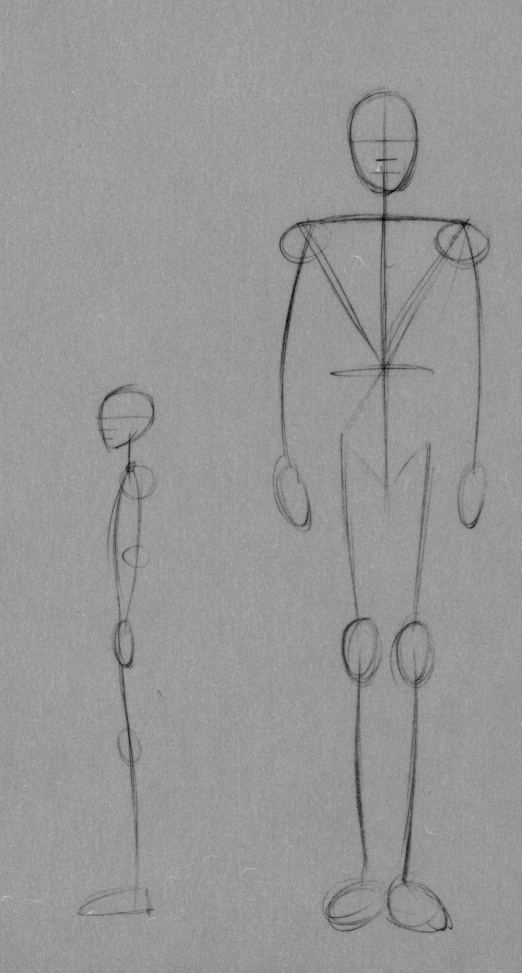

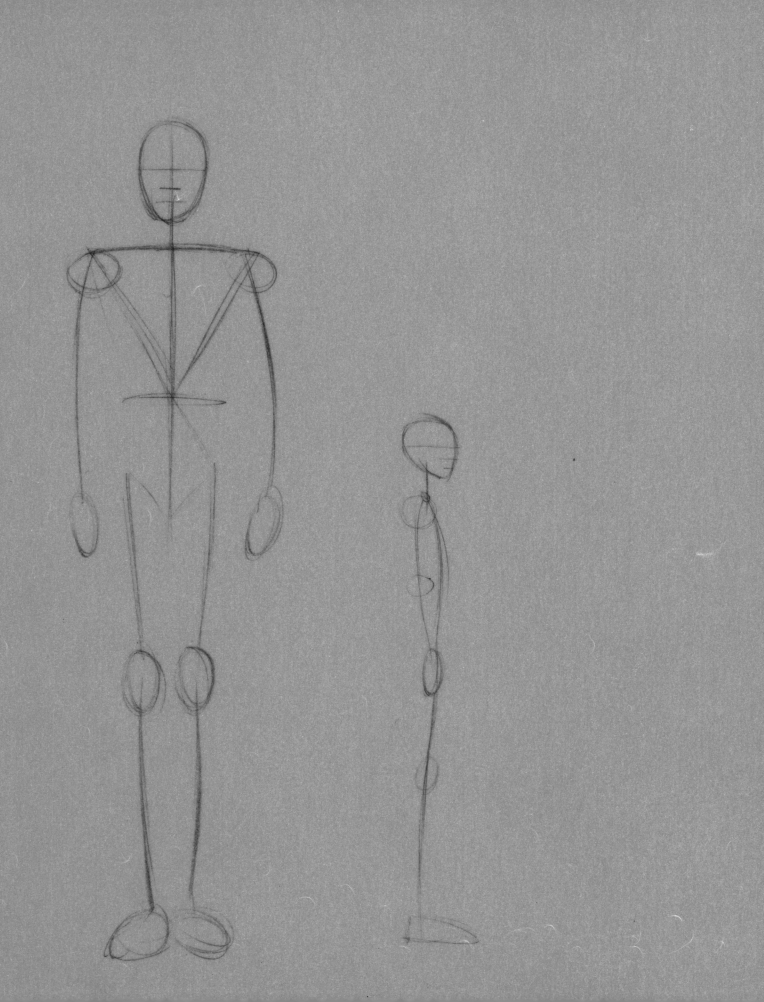

Sue Richards

Compared with Elektra or Storm, Sue Richards's uniform is quite plain and basic. It neatly fits her form but doesn't have any extras, like a cape or headwear. When you look at an illustration of Sue, her face and hair are striking because they are not covered by any item of costume. This makes her head and facial expressions very important for conveying drama and emotion.

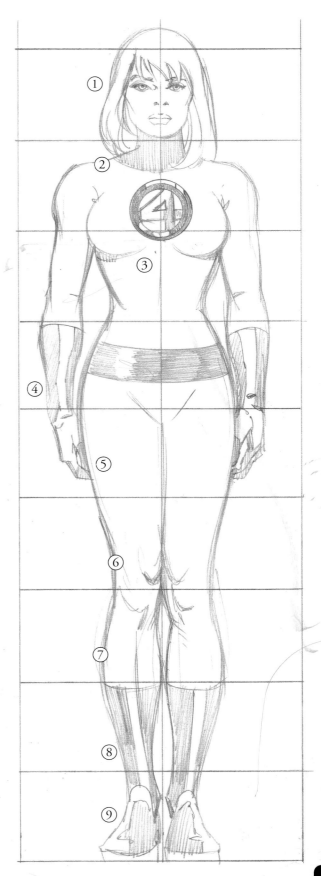

THE MEASUREMENTS

While the female figure is also nine heads high, she will usually be shorter and less muscular than the male figure. This is acheived by drawing her head just a bit smaller than a male's. Marvel's females are super-strong so they should have chisled shoulders, strong biceps, and powerful forearm.

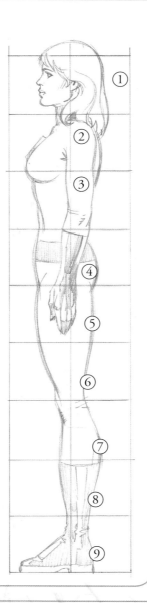

1. Draw a grid that is nine boxes high with a vertical axis. Rough in an oval for the head.

2. A female's shoulders are only about two heads wide compared to a male's, which are three heads wide.

3. The figure will widen a bit around the breast line and then narrow as you move down toward the waist.

4. The wrists should be narrower than a man's, but wider at the hips with a smooth curve.

5. The arms end at the hand and the hips blend smoothly into the thigh.

6. The narrowing, tapered effect continues as you work down into the knees.

7. Widen your figure a little bit as you work through the calves.

8. Taper into the lower shin…

9. … and end with the ankles and feet. Keep at it until it becomes easier to draw!

MUSCLE!

PACK A PUNCH

When looking at Marvel characters, one of the first things you will notice is how muscular they are. If you want people to believe your figure can punch through a brick wall, the correct physique is required. Muscles give your figure an appearance of mass and bulk that separates him or her from normal characters and gives a sense of power. Steel-like Colossus looks like he could lift an entire mountain. Why? Muscle on top of muscle on top of muscle!

YOUR TURN!

When you have read this section on muscles, go to the library or bookstore and have a look at books on basic anatomy. This will help you understand more fully how the body's muscles weave together. Try drawing parts of the body, such as a bicep, shoulder, or an entire arm in different positions. This will help you see how different muscles move and look.

MUSCULAR STRUCTURE

Muscles are fibrous or stringy in nature, with one muscle generally flowing into the next. In this example the shoulder muscle, or deltoid, flows into the biceps and triceps, which then flow into the twisting brachioradialis of the forearm. It sounds like a real mouthful, but it is all part of learning how to draw Super Heroes and villains. It won't be long before you are drawing biceps and triceps with ease!

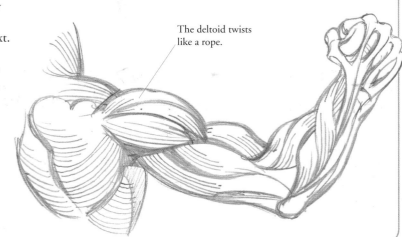

The deltoid twists like a rope.

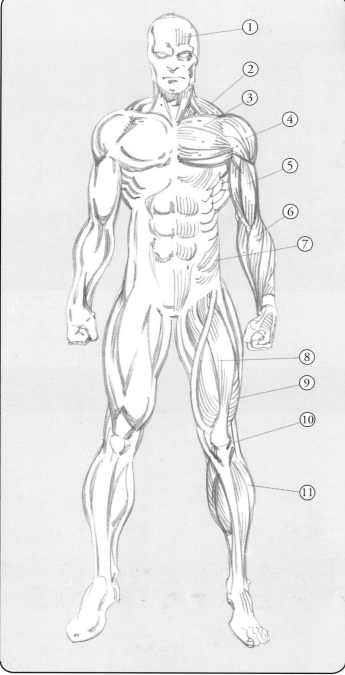

FRONT STRUCTURE

1. Frontalis
2. Trapezius
3. Pectoralis Major
4. Deltoid
5. Biceps
6. Brachioradialis
7. External Abdominal Oblique
8. Rectus Femoris
9. Vastus Lateralis
10. Sartorius
11. Peroneus Longus

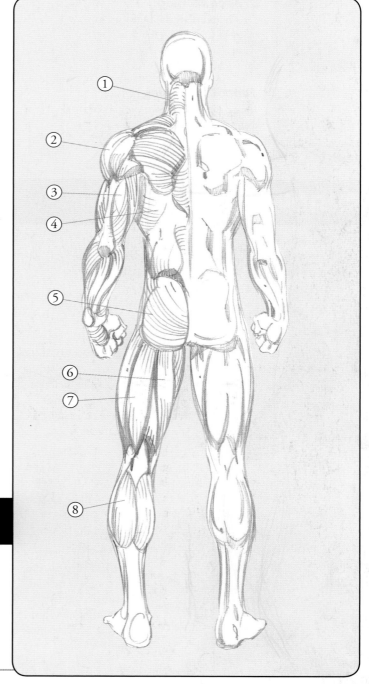

BACK STRUCTURE

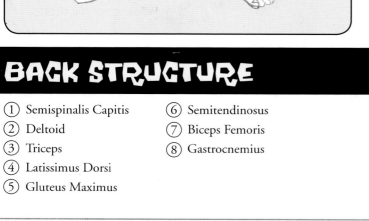

1. Semispinalis Capitis
2. Deltoid
3. Triceps
4. Latissimus Dorsi
5. Gluteus Maximus
6. Semitendinosus
7. Biceps Femoris
8. Gastrocnemius

SHADING

A SHADE FURTHER

Shading is the technique you use to give depth and dimension to your drawings by adding black tones. As you draw the outline of your character, the line suggests the form of the figure. If you vary the width of the line or darken a large portion of your figure, it will take on a feeling of weight that makes it seem more real.

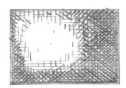

Crosshatching
Crosshatching is the build-up of layers of lines at angles to each other. The closer the lines are to each other, the darker the area.

Smooth shading
Using the side of your pencil gives a smooth effect. The tones can be defined by using your finger to smooth out the pencil work.

Kicking out
Captain America is a true action hero. In this illustration, the dark shading emphasizes his powerful muscles as he kicks out at his foe.

SHADING EFFECTS

The shading effects you choose will depend on where your light source is. Decide whether the light source is in front of, behind, to the side of, or below the object.

Above
This high-contrast look indicates a very strong source of light above and to the sphere's right. The shading is smooth and dark.

In front
This sphere is so dark that we can safely assume the light, to the front and right of the sphere, is distant or weak. The shading is darker around the edge of the sphere and is almost white at the top right.

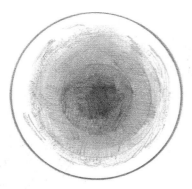

Behind
A diffused or spread-out effect suggests the light source is behind the sphere, gently highlighting the form. This is a good example of smooth shading.

In front and behind
Two sources of light, one in front and the other behind, create a rim effect that emphasizes the sphere's form. The shading stops at the top right, giving the sphere more depth.

SHADING FIGURES
This drawing of Wolverine looks far more finished on the left side of the picture where the shading indicates weight and depth.

STEP-BY-STEP

1) Rough Wolverine out first, using a stick figure and shapes, just like you did earlier!

2) Work in some of the muscle groups, like the biceps, to help to define the figure.

3) Give the figure depth by darkening individual parts of the costume.

4) Look at the dark line around Wolverine's outstretched arm. By "beefing up" the outline on the underside of his limbs, you can suggest shadow and weight.

Deadly dinosaurs
Wolverine is highly skilled in hand-to-hand combat. His claws make the battle more dramatic, especially in an exotic location like the Savage Land. Look at the contrast between his darkly shaded costume and his shining claws.

UNUSUAL SHAPES

ONE OF A KIND

Using unusual shapes or shapes that are out of proportion can be a very effective tool in creating a character with a unique look. In the same way that basketball players might be tall and angular, a truly massive character with great weight and mass suggests a rock-solid, immovable object.

HULK

Few characters are harder to move than the Hulk! He is still composed of basic shapes, like a more normal figure, but the arms, legs, and trunk are thicker and much larger. The Hulk is capable of running right through a concrete wall, so he has to look the part with arms, thighs, and hands that are far bigger than his head.

MARVEL EXPERT ADVICE

Whenever I draw a heavy, bulky character like the Hulk, I try to keep one thing in mind: just when I think I've made him big and strong enough, I have to make him even bigger and stronger! Lay on the muscles and bulk and you can't go wrong.

① The Hulk's pectoral muscles are broad and well defined, giving his upper body a sense of great width.

② His arms are far bigger than a normal man's thighs.

③ If the arms are big, the legs will be even bigger!

STEP-BY-STEP

UNUSUAL EFFECTS

Few characters are as much fun to draw as the Thing. He's thick, stocky, and looks like he is impossible to knock over.

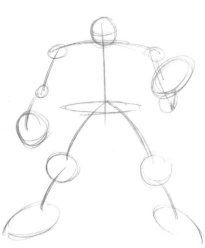

1) Firstly, rough out your character with a stick figure that features extra-wide shoulders and big hands and feet.

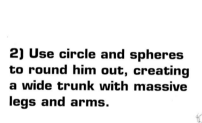

2) Use circle and spheres to round him out, creating a wide trunk with massive legs and arms.

3) The most important part of the Thing is his rock-like skin so try to add that. Rocks are heavy and angular. Remember this when you are finishing off this Fantastic character!

Strange and unusual

The Marvel universe is filled with figures of vastly different shapes and sizes. Have a go at drawing these characters or even creating your own.

ACTION!

ON THE MOVE

Any comic you pick up features still pictures, but it is the artist's job to keep those characters moving across the page. What fun would Spidey be if we couldn't see him swinging through the city? The idea is to get your character moving in the most dynamic and interesting way possible.

Speedy Spider-Man

Who has time to walk when they are busy saving the world? Most Marvel characters run, swing, or fly to their destinations. This rapid motion makes characters like Spider-Man special, whether wall-crawling or fighting off foes.

NIGHTCRAWLER

In this sequence, Nightcrawler leaps high into the air and lands, ready for action. Each drawing matches a particular stage of action and, when put together, suggests flowing, continuous motion.

1) He crouches, his muscles tense, ready to leap.

2) He leaps, with the upward motion clearly carrying him up and forward. Look at the line of his body from his left foot to his left hand.

3) At this point Nightcrawler appears to almost hang in mid-air, using his pointed tail to balance.

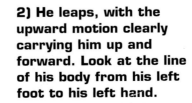

ACTION SKETCHBOOK

Every artist doodles figures and sketches during his or her spare time. Take a look at these sketches and imagine them as your favorite Marvel character. Then try your own, working quickly to capture the movement.

4) He begins to drop. He is fully in control and is ready to land.

5) Having avoided danger, he is on the ground again, ready and waiting to battle his enemies.

Nightmare
The shadows on Nightcrawler's face frame his eyes, making them really expressive. His pointed tail adds to his dark character.

ACTION DETAILS

TWISTS AND TURNS

When drawing a figure in action, it all starts with the twist and curve of the trunk. This gives the body a feel of motion and direction. The legs and arms can go off in different directions, but the trunk is your anchor. Simply drawing a basic stick figure with a curve gives a sense of dynamic motion.

Trunk rotation

The example below features the torso bent over in a "C" curve. Its name comes from the dark central axis line in the shape of the letter "C." The other torso (right) features a twisting motion, or "S" curve. Both are well balanced and it is easy to imagine the arms and legs drawn in a number of different ways.

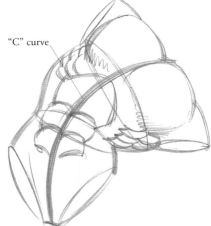

"C" curve

"S" curve

A Storm brewing

This drawing uses a reverse "C" curve. Storm's head tilts away from the curve. The shoulders angle with the curve but her hips are parallel to the ground.

SPEED LINES

Another tool used in Super Hero comics to create movement are speed lines. Try drawing Quicksilver in a dynamic running pose and he will look fast. However, if you add speed lines he becomes super-fast!

Speed line

The simple addition of speed lines around Iron Man make him look like he is zooming through the sky.

YOUR TURN!

Draw a stick figure using either the "C" or "S" curve technique and then flesh it out by adding the outline form, pectoral, and abdominal muscles. Lightly sketch the figure, adding the head, arms, and legs. Don't darken your lines until you are really happy with your drawing.

STEP-BY-STEP

UNDER PRESSURE
Dynamic tension is achieved when your figure is straining against multiple pressure points. In this example, the Black Panther is trying to break free.

4) Darken the shading to emphasize the effort. Don't forget to show the strain on his face too.

1) Make the axis line a reverse "C." The legs and arms will push in different directions.

2) Flesh out the body, increasing the muscle size to give the feeling of great effort as the Black Panther tries to push free.

3) Continue defining the muscles, showing the strain as they flex and push against the opposing force.

High flier
Though he has enhanced senses, Daredevil doesn't have a physical superpower. However, the way that he races across the roofs of New York and swings among the skyscrapers shows that he is a true Marvel action hero. His dramatic red costume stands out from the drab brown and gray city that he speeds through, and it helps to make Daredevil highly visible in the night sky.

PERSPECTIVE

SET THE SCENE
Now that you can draw figures, you will want to draw buildings for them to leap up and fly over! To do this, you'll need to learn about perspective. Put simply, perspective is the way that artists make drawings look three-dimensional. Don't worry—it's not too difficult once you've learned the basics.

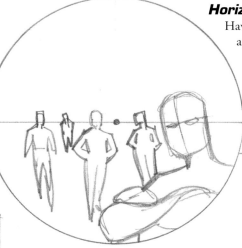

Horizons
Have you noticed how people appear to become smaller the further they are away from you? The furthest away they can still be seen is the horizon, drawn as a horizontal line. This line is the starting point for perspective.

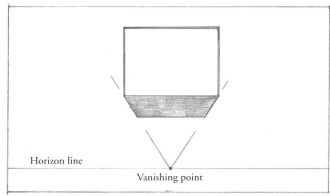

Horizon line

Vanishing point

One-point perspective
Try this—find a box and look at it front-on at eye level. It looks like a flat square or rectangle. But when you move it above your eyeline, you see the underside. Now look closely—the underside appears to become narrower toward the back (try closing one eye). If the left and right edges extended into the distance, they would get closer and closer and eventually meet. The point at which they meet is called the vanishing point. It sits on the horizon line. This is known as one-point perspective.

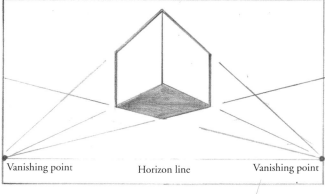

Vanishing point   Horizon line   Vanishing point

Two-point perspective
This time, we're still looking at the box from below, but it's rotated a little so we can see three of its sides. Again, look carefully at the side edges. All three sides look like they are narrowing to the left and right. The left edges would eventually meet at a vanishing point on the left and the right edges would meet at a point on the right. This is called two-point perspective. You could also work out how you would draw the box if you were looking down on it from above.

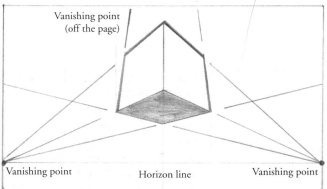

Vanishing point
(off the page)

Vanishing point   Horizon line   Vanishing point

Three-point perspective
Now move the box closer to you and tilt it a bit more. The sides will appear to narrow as they go upward. If you had a large enough piece of paper, they would eventually meet at a vanishing point way up above! Three-point perspective gives height to your picture. It's great to use for drawing skyscrapers. Look at the building on the opposite page and you will see three-point perspective in practice. Well done—you've learned all you need to know about perspective so let's get drawing!

IN ACTION

It is one thing to draw a building as though we are looking straight at it. It is quite another to take that same building and make it feel dynamic. This picture is in three-point perspective and conveys that dramatic feeling by creating tall, imposing buildings.

YOUR TURN!

Place three vanishing points on your board, outside the area in which you want to place your objects. Draw the lines from these points and sketch in buildings. Add detail until you are satisfied. Finish it off with Hulk or Spider-Man leaping through the scene!

CHARACTERS IN SCENES

People sometimes wonder what they should draw first: the background or their main character. It is better to form them at the same time so that the elements link together well.

1) Sketch in the buildings in three-point perspective. Make the figure of Spider-Man the central element.

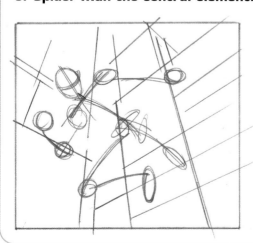

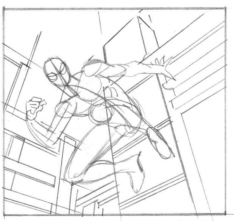

2) Sketch in some of the details of the building, such as windows, and flesh out Spidey.

3) Add shadows coming from both Spider-Man and the buildings. Experiment with different features of the buildings, like windows and brickwork. Remember to keep it all in perspective and you will have a great picture!

STEP-BY-STEP

BODY PERSPECTIVE

DON'T LOOK DOWN!

Until now your figure work has been rather conventional. But what happens if you are on a balcony looking down at Captain America? His appearance would be noticeably different, as this three-point perspective drawing shows. Perspective heightens the sense of drama for characters, just as it does for buildings.

Different angles

The benefits of perspective are shown by the two examples below. In both instances, Iron Man is walking into an exotic, high-tech lab. The first is a fairly conventional shot. The shot is technically correct, but the angle doesn't really dramatize the scene. The second shot is from below with lots of perspective on both Iron Man and the room, creating a more dynamic, dramatic shot.

PERSPECTIVE SKETCHBOOK

Here are a number of different poses using mixed perspective points. Trace these and then try some of your own, using various perspective points and basic shapes.

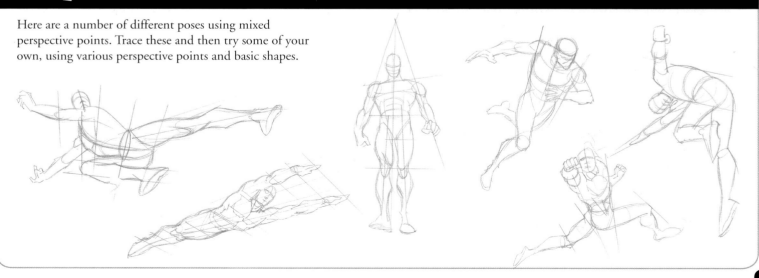

FORESHORTENING

ARM'S LENGTH

If you stand in front of a mirror and hold your arm out to the side and level with your shoulder, you can see it extends away from you. Turn until your arm is pointing at the mirror and you will see that it appears to be getting shorter. This is foreshortening.

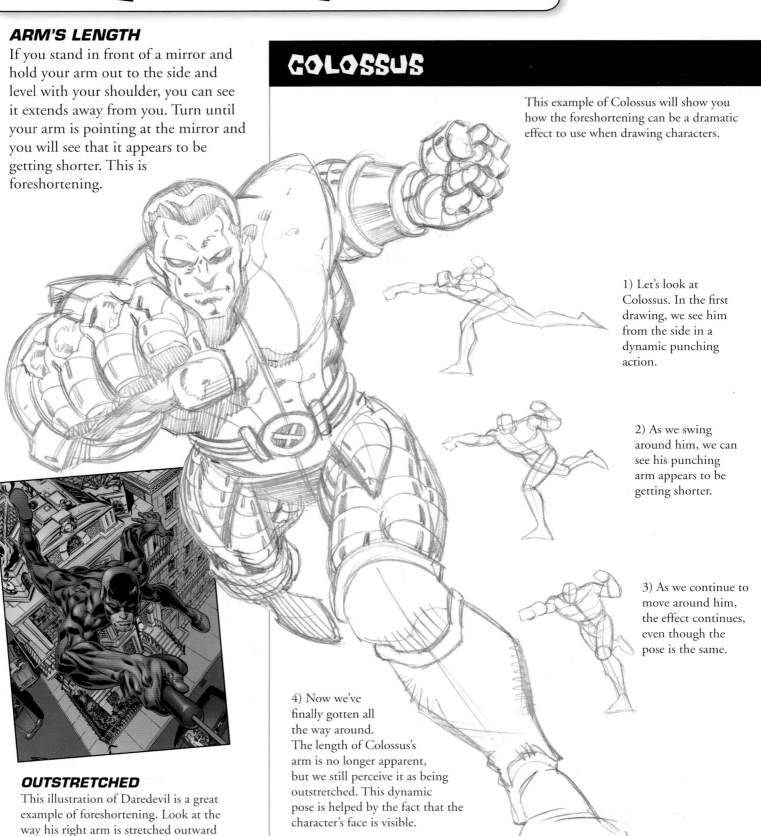

COLOSSUS

This example of Colossus will show you how the foreshortening can be a dramatic effect to use when drawing characters.

1) Let's look at Colossus. In the first drawing, we see him from the side in a dynamic punching action.

2) As we swing around him, we can see his punching arm appears to be getting shorter.

3) As we continue to move around him, the effect continues, even though the pose is the same.

4) Now we've finally gotten all the way around. The length of Colossus's arm is no longer apparent, but we still perceive it as being outstretched. This dynamic pose is helped by the fact that the character's face is visible.

OUTSTRETCHED

This illustration of Daredevil is a great example of foreshortening. Look at the way his right arm is stretched outward and his right leg is stretched backward.

STEP-BY-STEP

LONG AND THE SHORT OF IT

Foreshortening is hard to master, but the more you work at it, the more you'll see huge results. Think of the Black Widow in terms of basic shapes and it will be much easier.

1) Let's say we want a cool shot of Black Widow delivering a solid kick. Start with a stick figure, getting the bottom of the kicking foot up close to the head.

2) Work through the body. Visualizing or thinking of the leg as two foreshortened cylinders will help you.

3) Now that you've laid down the basic form you can add detail and costuming to finish.

MARVEL EXPERT ADVICE

When you try to draw a foreshortened pose, it helps to sketch it first from the side, just as we did on the previous page, to see how the limbs and trunk connect. If you then redraw that same figure from a more dynamic angle it will give you a great result. Practice different effects by stretching out your arm in front of the mirror. Move your arm back and forth, and up and down, looking at the way the foreshortening angles change.

Black Widow

The Black Widow doesn't have any superpowers but she is a highly skilled spy. Her wrist cartridges contain tools that she needs for her work, including tear-gas pellets, a spring-loaded cable, and a device capable of giving off electrostatic charges. Tiny suction cups built into her uniform help the Widow walk on walls and ceilings. If you want to show her crawling along the wall toward the reader, you should use your foreshortening skills.

SPIDER-MAN

World-famous web-slinger, Spider-Man is a sticky figure to pin down. He is super-strong, with well-developed leg muscles due to his ability to jump whole blocks in one leap. He is frequently seen in spider pose, crouched low as he scales buildings. The web-shooters are an important part of Spidey's costume. They project web fluid that creates a strong fibre, letting him spin webs and swing from skyscraper to skyscraper. Spider-Man is also incredibly fast and agile and is often seen speeding through New York. Spider-Man's athletic body shape and characteristic costume means you will need to use all you have learnt about body structure and costumes to draw this classic Marvel Super Hero!

AMAZING FANTASY #15
In August 1962 a very different Super Hero burst on to the scene—Spider-Man! This cover shows a characteristic image of Spidey swinging through the cityscape. (Cover art by Jack Kirby)

CHARACTER HISTORY

Studious Peter Parker lived with his Uncle Ben and Aunt May in New York City. One evening he attended an exhibition on nuclear laboratory waste and was bitten by a spider that had been exposed to radiation. In pain, Parker left the exhibition and was attacked by a gang. A dramatic surge of strength allowed him to defend himself and he escaped, scaling a nearby wall and sticking to it with his fingertips! Parker realized these new powers were a direct result of the spider bite. He decided to compete as a wrestler to test his new powers and donned a mask to disguise himself. Calling himself the Amazing Spider-Man, his popularity grew and he created a colorful costume for himself. Using his scientific skills, Peter also made a special web fluid and web-shooters to enhance

his spider-like abilities. Following an appearance on television, Parker allowed a burglar to escape when he could have stopped him. This would come back to haunt him as the burglar went on to kill Peter's beloved Uncle Ben. Suddenly Peter's perception of his powers changed. Realizing that with great power comes great responsibility, he vowed to use his powers for the greater good. And so was born the truly Amazing Spider-Man, one of the most famous Super Heroes of all time.

BECOMING SPIDER-MAN

This illustration captures the moment when Peter Parker's life would change forever.

MARVEL EXPERT ADVICE

Spider-Man is one of the most visually interesting characters ever invented. His flexible poses are unique. Positions and stances that would be wrong for any other character make Spidey even more bug-like. You can have great fun with this Super Hero. Bend him, shape him, and twist him any way that you want. Chances are if you do this, your drawing will be more exciting.

ROUGH PENCIL DRAWING

First, imagine the pose that you want. When drawing Spider-Man, work fast so that the figure stays loose and flexible. Even at this early stage, this simple stick figure, rounded out with cylinders, is clearly Spidey.

FINAL PENCIL DRAWING

Next, you should finalize the body, legs, and arms, and add muscle detail. Then start on the costume. Take your time on the webbing. It is easiest to start with his mask, extending through the arms and chest.

The webs on Spidey's costume originate in his mask and extend through his body.

Keep Spidey slender and not too muscular.

Use the foreshortening techniques you have learnt to draw Spider-Man springing into action.

VILLAINS

No Marvel hero has a better group of villains than Spider-Man. There's Mysterio, Venom, Carnage, the Lizard, and many others who make Spider-Man's life miserable. And don't forget the maniacal Green Goblin who killed Spider-Man's beloved Gwen Stacy. One of the most visually striking is Dr Octopus, a twisted genius whose monstrous arms can rip a tank apart.

Doc Ock's mechanical arms make him one of Spidey's greatest foes. Try to capture the texture of these titanium tentacles.

SPIDER-SENSE

The radioactive spider that bit Peter Parker gave him more than great strength and the ability to stick to walls. It also gave him spider-sense, a unique early warning system that alerts Spider-Man to impending danger. It's saved him from danger many times!

WALL-CRAWLER

Like a real spider, Spider-Man can cling to virtually any surface, no matter how slick. He crouches down close to the wall and spreads his fingers wide to maintain his grip as he creeps up on his foes.

WEBS

Spider-Man uses the webbing that he created as Peter Parker to swing through the streets of New York City. He launches the webbing out of his wrist-mounted web-shooters and wears extra web cartridges on his belt. Although Spider-Man is not as muscular as the Hulk, his muscles are clearly visible as he flies through the city. The dark inking emphasizes these muscles.

Showing the long strings of webbing can give a real sense of perspective to the picture.

FINAL INKED DRAWING

Your inked figure should make a strong impression. Inking creates a more graphic image than your original pencil art. Add larger areas of black to parts of the costume, especially the arms, to give the figure more weight. Well done—you've drawn a striking Spider-Man!

Space the web lines out so that they don't bleed together.

Use dark shadows to give your figure depth.

BATTLE!

FIGHT NIGHT

What good are Super Heroes if they don't have someone to fight? To create a fight scene, you'll need to draw at least two characters and put them in a proper setting. Look at this classic Marvel fight scene and use the trace overlay to see what makes it work. After that, have a go at making your own scene featuring your favorite characters.

THE HEAD

FROM THE TOP

Now we'll work on specifics, starting with the head. The face communicates emotion and intent while revealing the individual's true nature. There are some very basic tips to help you draw the most important aspect of your character.

STEP-BY-STEP

HEAD START

To draw Wolverine's head or any other character's, it is best to start with a simple, forward view, as though our character is standing right in front of us. We'll begin with a basic oval.

1) Draw your oval with the large side at the top, like an upside-down egg. Divide the face in half vertically to center your features.

2) Draw three horizontal lines: one will position the eyes, one will show where the nose is, and the last one represents the mouth.

3) Keep working, roughing in the nose, eyes, and mouth, and adding the ears. The tops of the ears should be in line with the eyes.

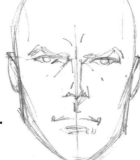

STRUCTURE OF THE FACE

The skull defines the basic shape of an individual's head, the angle of the jaw, and width and height of the forehead. Soft tissue and flexible tissue called cartilage define the shape of the nose, while muscles control facial movement and expression.

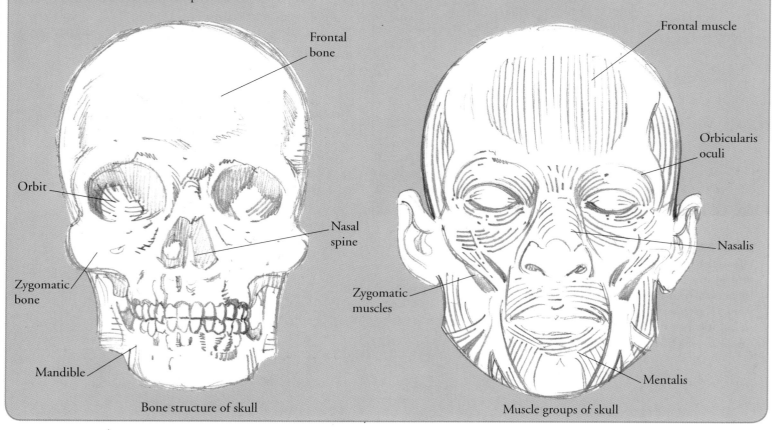

Frontal bone

Orbit

Nasal spine

Zygomatic bone

Mandible

Bone structure of skull

Frontal muscle

Orbicularis oculi

Nasalis

Zygomatic muscles

Mentalis

Muscle groups of skull

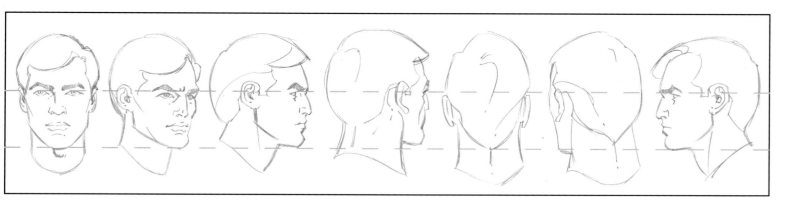

Planes of the face

These "turnarounds" show that it is possible to keep the look and style of a character no matter where you are viewing the individual from. On the following page, you will learn how to draw the head in profile or side-on. Comic-book artists draw their figures in a variety of poses over the course of a story, so keeping them in character is important.

MALE HEAD

ON THE FACE OF IT

Now that you have the basics, we will focus on a classic, heroic male face. This means that the face will have symmetrical features and proportions, a classically sculpted jaw, and a strong nose. Combine all of these details with a cool hairstyle and you're beginning to master how to draw a Marvel Super Hero!

Heads up

Thor is the god of thunder and he should always display that grand status in the way that he stands and in his facial expressions. He has a chisled face, with strong nose and jawline, and long, flowing hair, which all add to his noble and distinguished look.

STEP-BY-STEP

CLASSIC MALE HEAD

We used a grid for the body and we'll do the same with the head to keep the face in proportion. We'll start in a similar way to the way we drew the head on the previous page. Using a rectangle as an outline will help with the proportions.

1) Halve a rectangle with a vertical line. Add the three horizontal lines to show the eyes, nose, and mouth, as you did before.

2) Fill out the eyes, nose, and mouth and indicate the shape of the jaw. You can also start to show detail, like the eyebrows.

3) Finish off by finalizing the details and adding ears and hair. Wavy lines can give the hair body and show the style. Notice the lines that emphasize the strong structure of the Marvel male face. Good job!

STEP-BY-STEP

PROFILE

To draw the head in profile, start with a wider rectangle than you used for the front view. Sketch in the lines for the eyes, nose, and mouth.

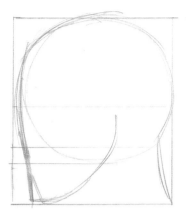

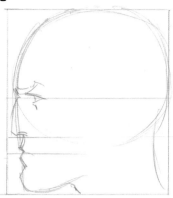

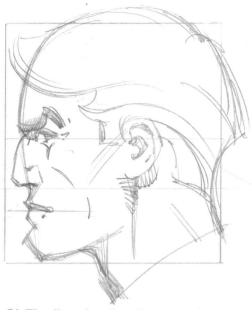

1) Rough in the shape of the head. The nose line will also show where the bottom of the ears will be.

2) Add the nose, mouth, eyes, and eyebrows. As this drawing is in profile, you can show the true depth of the eyes.

3) Finalize the details and define the shape of the jaw and chin. Finish the head with the hair and ears. In profile, you can see the ear in detail.

Male details

The male face is typically defined with thin lips, a strong nose, narrow eyes, and bushy eyebrows. Like everything else we've done, these can be constructed with simple shapes.

Mouth

Start with two long, angled triangular shapes. The bottom one should be slightly larger. Soften the features as you finish drawing. Shade the lips and make the bottom lip slightly fuller.

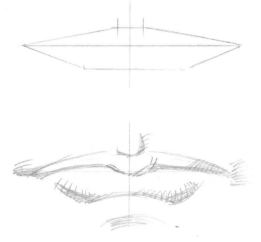

Nose

Start with a long, vertical rectangle and add triangles at the sides and bottom to give dimension. As you soften the lines, you will see that the lower triangles form the nostrils.

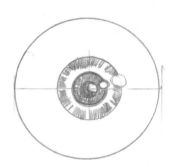

Eyes

Start with a circle for the eyeball, with a smaller one inside for the pupil. Use your shading skills here. Then draw a curve above and below the pupil. This will be the eyelid. Finish off with short eyelashes.

FEMALE HEAD

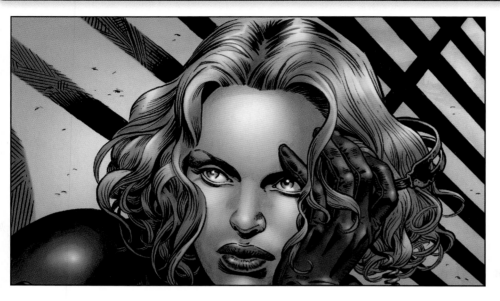

FACE OFF

Now that you've mastered the male head, it's time to shift gears for a classic, heroic female face. Like a man, her features should be symmetrical and in proportion, though the lines you use will be softer and graceful. Women have a greater variety of hairstyles than men so you have many options to choose from to create your Marvel heroine.

Turning heads

The Black Widow has a classic Marvel face, with shaped eyebrows, a slender nose, and full lips. Compare this with Thor on the previous page and you will see that the features are softer.

STEP-BY-STEP

CLASSIC FEMALE HEAD

Once again, we start with a grid to maintain proportion. Draw a rectangle, halving it with a vertical line. Add a horizontal line halfway up to mark the centerline of the eyes. You should be an expert at this!

1) Lightly sketch the shape of the head. The jaw line should taper to a narrower chin than you drew for the male head.

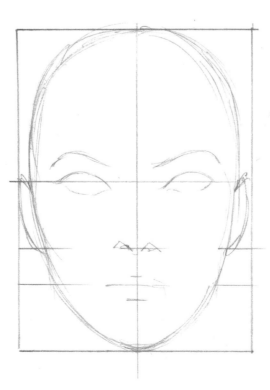

2) Add larger eyes, longer lashes, a slimmer nose, and fuller lips than you did for the man.

3) Finalize the facial features, adding ears and hair to finish your drawing. Notice how the female eyes are open and the eyebrows are trim and shaped.

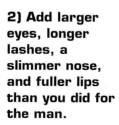

PROFILE

The female profile shot also uses softer features, more graceful lines, and a less angular approach to the face.

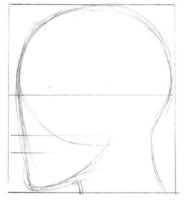

1) Start with a rectangle, adding horizontal lines for the eyes, nose, and mouth. Rough in the head shape.

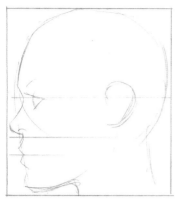

2) Add the nose, which shouldn't be as large as the male's, a mouth with full lips, large eyes, and neat eyebrows.

3) Finish your drawing with long eyelashes and whichever hairstyle you think your character would have!

Female details

As with the male head, we will use basic shapes to build the female features. However, the woman's lips and eyes will be a bit larger than the man's, while her nose will be more graceful.

Mouth

Use the triangular shapes again. Build the lips a bit higher than a man's so that they are not as wide but are fuller. Soften them as you finish.

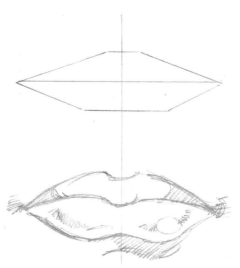

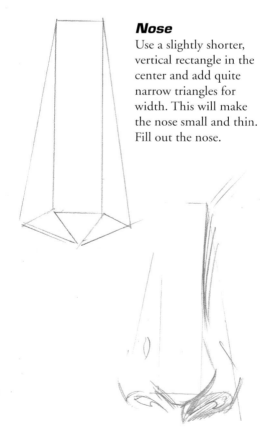

Nose

Use a slightly shorter, vertical rectangle in the center and add quite narrow triangles for width. This will make the nose small and thin. Fill out the nose.

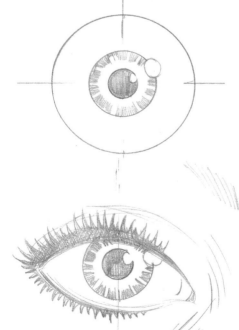

Eyes

Start with a circle for the eyeball and add a smaller one inside for the pupil. The eyelids surround the eye. Then you can draw in the long, curving eyelashes.

47

DRAMATIC LIGHT

IN THE DARK

The use of light and shadow in drawing can accomplish a number of things. A well-placed shadow adds true depth and a feeling of dimension to your work. A figure cloaked in shadow can give a drawing a foreboding feeling of danger.

Green with envy

The Green Goblin is considered to be Spider-Man's deadliest foe. He's even more menacing under the glow of a full moon.

STEP-BY-STEP

DARK SHADOWS

Green Goblin has a unique face and is a good example to use to show how shadows can affect the look, emphasizing his threatening appearance.

1) Rough out the general shape of the head. You can start planning where the shadows will be but don't add them yet.

2) Choose your lighting source as this will determine where your shadow will fall. Here the light is coming in at the left side of the picture.

3) Fill out the shading. Make it fairly dark to give the head menace. With the shading completed, your foe has dimension and a truly evil appearance.

In the dark

This shot of Daredevil uses shadows in a graphic way. The intense shadows make him look like a mysterious creature of the city. Even in the dark, his red costume jumps off the page.

Under the head

In this first example, the light source is directly under the face, as though the character is holding a flashlight. This gives him an eerie, somewhat evil appearance.

Light sources

Have you ever wondered what happens if you draw the exact same face several times and change the light source? These examples show how the results can vary dramatically .

Above the head

Now the light has moved above so that it is shining down hard on the head. The brow casts shadows that obscure the eyes while the nose, cheekbones, and chin give off shadows as well.

To the side of the head

In this shot the light has been moved over to the right of the picture. The nose casts a shadow that sweeps to the left where the entire head is in shadow.

YOUR TURN!

Use a flashlight and stand in front of a mirror. Move the flashlight around your head, away from it, and closer toward it. Experiment with lots of different angles to see the different effects that you can achieve. Watch the shadows on your face change as you move the light to different places. See if you can create the effects that are shown above with your flashlight.

HANDS

HANDS ON

It is easy to see that a face is expressive. You may not realize it, but hands are too. A fist implies threat. An open palmed hand implies friendship. Hands are difficult to draw, but every character has them, so let's get to work!

HAND STRUCTURE

The structure of the skeleton for male and female hands is very similar, but a man's hand tends to be a bit wider with more obvious knuckles and thicker fingers. A woman's hand is more graceful and slender, often with longer, shaped fingernails.

Female hand

Male hand

Metacarpal bones

Hamate

Scaphoid

Radius

Ulna

Carpal bones

The top of the thumb lines up with the base of the fingers.

IN THE PALM OF YOUR HAND

You can probably recognize the shapes you will need to construct a hand. For instance, a finger looks exactly like a cylinder.

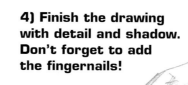

1) Draw a horizontal line halfway down the side of a rectangle, to indicate the wrist. The rectangle is the palm of the hand.

2) Draw the centerlines for each finger and the thumb to show their positions.

3) Flesh the fingers out with cylinder shapes. Use circles to give the effect of the palm.

4) Finish the drawing with detail and shadow. Don't forget to add the fingernails!

Fists

Make a fist and take a good look at it. Notice how your four fingers bend in to the palm while your thumb wraps around them.

1) From the front, a fist looks like this, with the fingers in line with the knuckles.

2) A side view shows how the index finger bends in, allowing the thumb to wrap around it.

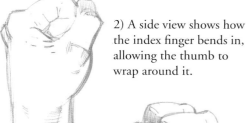

3) A ¾ view is the best, showing all aspects of the four fingers and thumb working together.

GRIP

In this drawing, Thor's hand follows the same general rule of the thumb wrapping around the fingers, but the fingers aren't closed tight to the palm. Their distance from the palm is determined by the size of the hammer that Thor is holding.

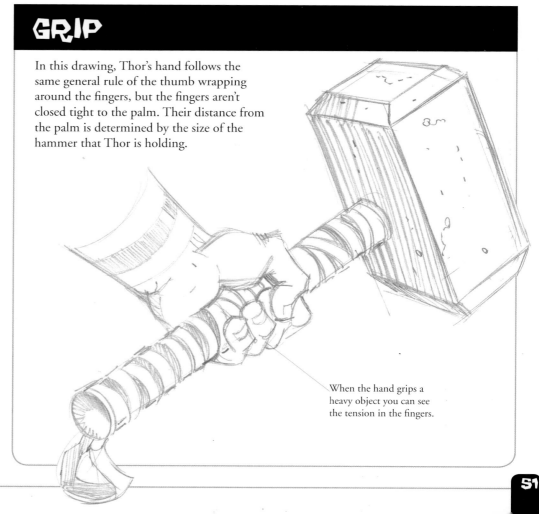

When the hand grips a heavy object you can see the tension in the fingers.

FEET

FEET ON THE GROUND

Most of the people you draw will be wearing shoes or boots but it is still important to learn how to draw the human foot. The foot does not have to move into as many positions as the hand but it still moves and flexes. This means that your approach will be similar to the one used for the hand.

FOOT STRUCTURE

It may seem obvious that the foot can be found at the bottom of the leg, but it is worth knowing how it all connects together. The tibia is the main bone in the lower leg with the slightly smaller fibula, ending at the ankle.

Femur

Calf muscles tend to be large in Marvel figures

Fibula

Tibia

Tarsals

Metatarsals

Phalanges

Flight of fancy

Prince Namor comes from the underwater realm of Atlantis so naturally he doesn't wear shoes! The wings on his ankles might be small but they give him the ability to fly.

PUT YOUR FOOT DOWN!

The leg and foot are represented by a cylinder connected to a rectangle. The foot flexes at the ankle, so you can change the angle of the leg as it bends to or away from the toes.

1) Start with a simple line marking the center of the leg attached to a rounded-off rectangle for the foot.

2) Flesh out the lower leg and heel, while indicating the five toes. Remember, they are much shorter than fingers.

3) Flesh out the toes and use shading to give the foot a fleshy look. Adding the bone at the ankle and the joints on the toes will make the foot look fantastic from top to toe!

Feet angles

Here are several feet drawn from a variety of angles. Pay particular attention to the way that the feet flex and the legs stretch.

Footprints

A walk on the beach or a step in wet cement will leave footprints. They will look like the bottom of the foot, only messier and less defined. Look for the details that make them recognizable as footprints.

CLOTHING

DRESS TO IMPRESS

Now you know how to draw the body, you need to learn how to draw what covers it! You will learn the essential techniques required to draw any sort of clothing, whether it's Bruce Banner's shirt tearing to shreds as he transforms into the Hulk, or Storm's flowing cape as she flies to the rescue.

Creases

In the drawing above, look at the way the shirt's wrinkles point to the inside of the arm. Think of this as a stress point from which creases emerge.

Rolled-up sleeves create folds in the material

On the case

Cigar in hand, J. Jonah Jameson strides through the *Daily Bugle* offices with attitude. Large, brisk steps make more wrinkles in the clothing and cause the pants to drape and wave.

Womenswear

The differences between male and female body shapes affect the way that the clothes hang and the appearance of the folds.

YOUR TURN!

If you want to draw Spider-Man hanging from the ceiling, you won't find much inspiration at home! But if you want to draw an ordinary person, home is the place to start. Ask a parent or sibling to sit while you draw them. Pay attention to the way their clothes look on them.

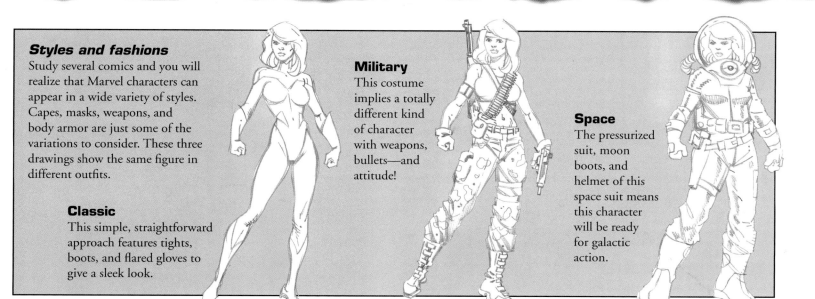

Styles and fashions

Study several comics and you will realize that Marvel characters can appear in a wide variety of styles. Capes, masks, weapons, and body armor are just some of the variations to consider. These three drawings show the same figure in different outfits.

Classic

This simple, straightforward approach features tights, boots, and flared gloves to give a sleek look.

Military

This costume implies a totally different kind of character with weapons, bullets—and attitude!

Space

The pressurized suit, moon boots, and helmet of this space suit means this character will be ready for galactic action.

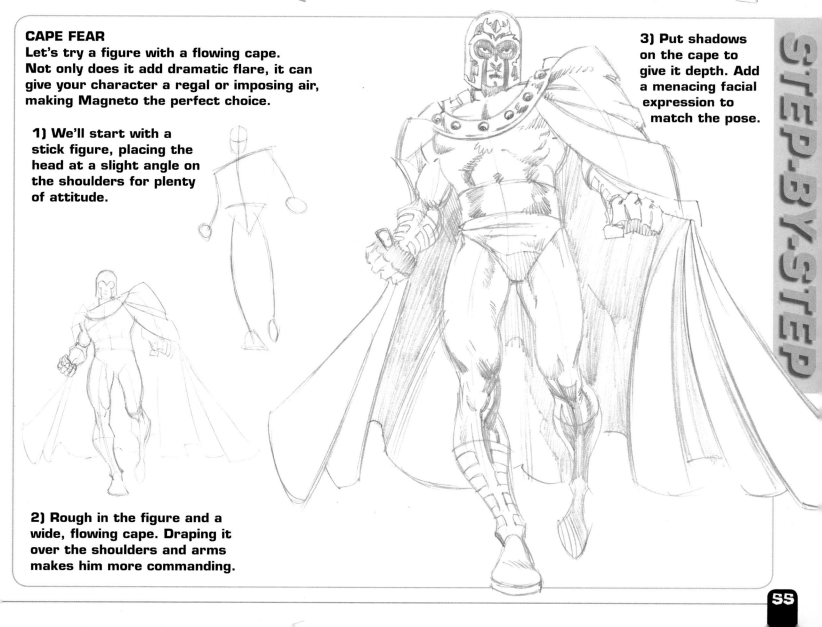

CAPE FEAR

Let's try a figure with a flowing cape. Not only does it add dramatic flare, it can give your character a regal or imposing air, making Magneto the perfect choice.

1) We'll start with a stick figure, placing the head at a slight angle on the shoulders for plenty of attitude.

2) Rough in the figure and a wide, flowing cape. Draping it over the shoulders and arms makes him more commanding.

3) Put shadows on the cape to give it depth. Add a menacing facial expression to match the pose.

STEP-BY-STEP

VILLAINS

THE GOOD, THE BAD, AND THE UGLY

Until now, we have mainly been drawing Super Heroes. However, villains can be even more fun to draw! The basics about body structure, heads, and costume are the same, but bad guys and girls tend to have zanier personalities, wilder costumes, and a sense of style that heroes don't always possess!

HEAD VILLAINS

Most heroes have textbook good looks but villains, like Dr Doom, can have crazy, distinct facial features. For the artist, this is the chance to have a bit more fun!

Mystique
If her general expression isn't enough to make you realize she's evil, the skull on her forehead certainly is.

Kingpin
A fairly normal face, but one with lots of bulk! The Kingpin is all about presence and power, which is always fun to capture.

Dr Octopus
Doc Ock's looks are quite nerdy. So, making him seem evil as well is part of the challenge.

ATTITUDE

The most important characteristic that villains have in common with each other is attitude. This can be shown through body posture and facial expression. Individuals like Sabretooth believe they are completely impossible to beat!

1. Wild hair, masks, exotic helmets, and threatening expressions are common among bad guys—and girls!

2. These characters are often bigger than the heroes they fight and have builds that look unstoppable.

3. Many of these villains need the edge to triumph over Super Heroes. Claws, knives, swords, and guns help along the way.

Villainous figures
This picture shows a number of different physical types and features. Look at gigantic Juggernaut, the Vulture's wings, and Sabretooth's claws. Use some of these ideas to sketch your own villains.

MARVEL EXPERT ADVICE

I'm often asked how I get ideas for villains. Much of that depends on the hero. If you're trying to dream up someone to fight Spider-Man, for example, you probably want your bad guy to have the ability to fly or scale walls. If you need someone to fight the Thing, your character will need a massive build with muscles to match.

MONSTERS

BEASTLY BEINGS

Comics are the perfect place to find really great monster stories. One of the best things about drawing monsters is that there's really no wrong way to do it. A monster can be as wild as you can possibly imagine, so go ahead and let your imagination run wild!

Fantastic fight

The Fantastic Four are battling with the Mole Man's monsters. The strange shapes and features of these beasts make it clear that they are monsters. It helps that the Fantastic Four can fight monsters with their very own—the Thing.

TRANSFORMATION

One of the most interesting types of monsters is the one that starts off as a human. No one shows that transformation better than Bruce Banner who becomes... the Hulk!

2) As he changes, his brow grows, his arms and legs thicken, and his chest expands.

3) Soon he's the Hulk—far more massive, heavier, and much, much stronger than that puny human Banner!

1) Bruce Banner is a fairly small, skinny person and is not at all threatening.

Monster features

To get you started, we'll look at a few details your monster might have. There are more features than these, but what you decide to use is determined by what is scary to you.

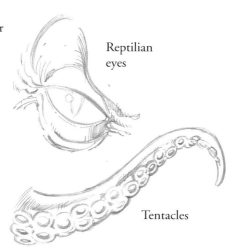

Reptilian eyes

Horns

Claws

Tentacles

YOUR **TURN!**

As you design your own monsters, consider the animal kingdom. Animals can have tails, sharp claws, scaly skin, and wings. You see all of these things on monsters as well. Mix these details in with some of your own ideas to build the coolest-ever monster.

REPTILES

Let's try drawing some of these details. We will use Spider-Man's classic foe, the Lizard.

1) Like all of our figurework, we will start with a basic stick figure to get the general pose. His head sits directly on his shoulders.

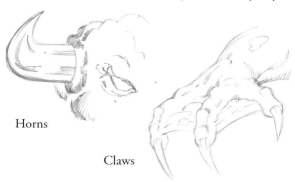

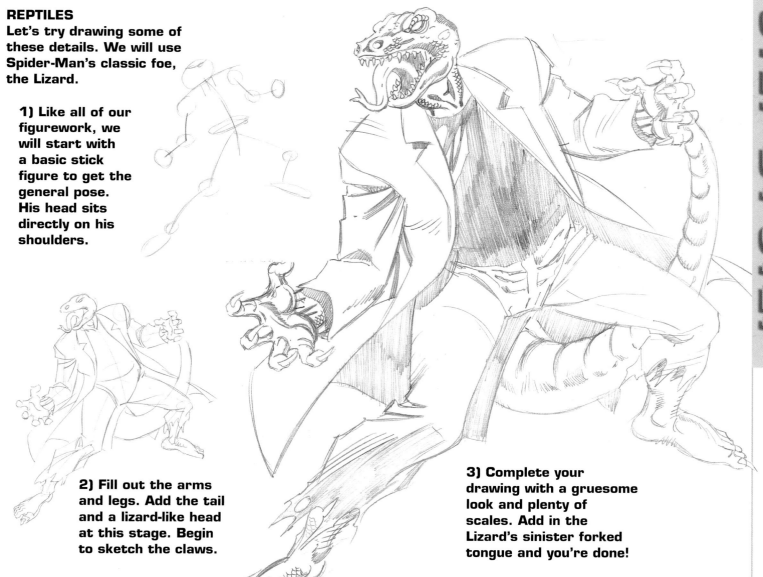

2) Fill out the arms and legs. Add the tail and a lizard-like head at this stage. Begin to sketch the claws.

3) Complete your drawing with a gruesome look and plenty of scales. Add in the Lizard's sinister forked tongue and you're done!

STEP-BY-STEP

EXCITING EXTRAS

HELPING HAND

Captain America carries a shield. Thor carries a hammer. Spider-Man has his web-shooters. The Punisher carries a whole arsenal of weapons! There is a long tradition of characters carrying all the equipment that they need in their fight for justice.

At the ready
Hunting vampires means that Blade needs to be ready with a selection of weapons.

WEAPONS

Heroes and villains alike carry weapons but we will look at just a few of the good guys' weapons of choice. As you design your own Super Hero, think about using these or other equipment to give them a unique look.

Grenade launcher

Anti-personnel grenade

Throwing knife

Machine gun

Throwing star (shuriken)

Captain America's shield

Automatic pistol

Thor's hammer

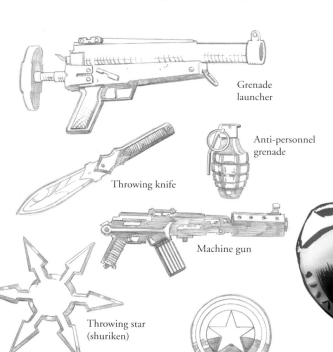

Vehicles

Everybody needs a way to get around. Blade and Ghost Rider both ride monster motorcycles and the X-Men have a powerful jet called Blackbird. If your character cannot fly or run at super-speed, you may want to give him or her a totally cool way to travel.

YOUR TURN!

Pick your favorite Marvel character and design a vehicle for him or her. Can it go anywhere? Fly? Drive up the side of a mountain? Is the owner's identity hidden or does it have an identifier—like Captain America's shield—emblazoned on the side?

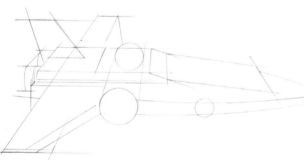

1) Start with basic shapes, using circles, triangles, and rectangles to construct the ship.

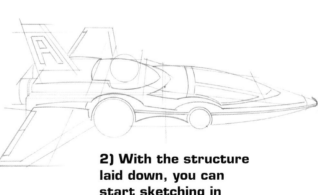

2) With the structure laid down, you can start sketching in the detail.

HIGH IN THE SKY
The Avengers travel the universe in the exotic Quinjet, a plane so cool we'd all love to take it for a test flight!

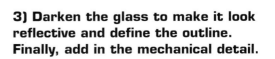

3) Darken the glass to make it look reflective and define the outline. Finally, add in the mechanical detail.

STEP-BY-STEP

STORM

Trained by fellow X-Men member Wolverine, Storm is a real force of nature. She can control the weather, causing downpours of snow and hail and producing typhoons and hurricanes. She creates winds that can carry her through the air and she is often seen in flight with her cape billowing behind her. Her main weapon is the ability to project electrical bolts from her hands at her enemies. She is also a highly skilled hand-to-hand combatant. Her white hair, blue eyes that often glow bright white, and lightning bolt earrings make her a striking individual.

CHARACTER HISTORY

Storm was born Ororo Munroe to David Munroe and N'Dare, a princess of a Kenyan tribe. N'Dare was descended from African priestesses who had white hair and blue eyes, characteristics Ororo would inherit. The family moved to Egypt, but when Ororo was young her parents were killed when their house was bombed. Ororo was left trapped under the rubble, which resulted in a lifelong fear of enclosed spaces. She wandered the streets until she was befriended by Achmed el-Gibar, who taught her how to pickpocket and steal. Professor Xavier and Storm's paths crossed in Egypt when she tried to pickpocket from him. When she was 12 years old, Storm left Egypt to visit her ancestor's homeland in the Serengeti Plains. On her journey Ororo discovered that she could control the weather, creating powerful storms of hail, snow, and thunder and lightning. These mutant powers were affected by her emotions, however, and a surge of anger could lead to a devastating storm. When she arrived at the Plains, she used her powers to help the farming tribes and was worshipped as a goddess by them. Some years later, Professor Xavier invited Ororo to join the X-Men and gave her the code name "Storm." Storm has used her powers ever since, for the good of all humanity.

UNIQUE LOOKS

Ororo's white hair and blue eyes made her—and Storm—distinctive individuals.

X-MEN #94
In August 1975, the "new" X-Men got their own series. This illustration shows Storm, Cyclops, Colossus, Banshee, and Nightcrawler being blasted to their doom by Nefaria. (Cover art by Gill Kane and Dave Cockrum)

MARVEL EXPERT ADVICE

Storm possesses a unique, almost regal look that makes her fun to draw. She should have a sense of presence on the page, as though she is in control of virtually any situation. She always stands tall and is graceful and majestic. This should show through in your illustration. If you were to draw Storm in a crouching Spider-Man pose it would be out of character.

ROUGH PENCIL DRAWING

In this pose, Storm is using her power to control the weather. The shot is straight-on, which stresses her height. If you draw her slightly curving to the side, the illustration is more dynamic than a simple standing pose. Use foreshortening to emphasize her outstretched arms.

FINAL PENCIL DRAWING

Finish the figure, fleshing it out with muscle and adding Storm's striking hair and facial details. Work in the costume details, such as her cape. Add shading, using black tones to draw attention to the curve of the figure.

Storm's hair is long with a styled look.

A character's cape can help create the impression of movement.

POWERS

Storm is a mutant with the ability to manipulate the weather. Capturing all these different environments, whether they are snowstorms, torrential rain, or thunder and lightning, is always exciting. In this picture, strobes of lightning are fired from her hands and her eyes flash white. However, she always stands strong and controlled. She knows that if she lets her emotions get out of control, catastrophic weather and storms will follow.

GODDESS

When Ororo N'Dare was living in the Serengeti Plains she was worshipped by the native people for her ability to control the weather. They believed that she must be a goddess as she was obviously able to tame Mother Nature. Now as Storm, she still stands in a regal, goddess-like manner. Her long limbs, muscles, and flowing cape add to her height and stature.

Storm's white hair and height make an immediate impression

CLASSICAL BEAUTY

With her height and grace, Storm is a classically beautiful woman. You can show the character and personality traits of figures by the way that you draw them. When drawing Storm, it is best to remember that she is a bit reserved and formal. For example, at a party she will usually stand tall rather than lean on a table.

FINAL INKED DRAWING

Now, ink the outline of Storm's figure and then blacken her cape to avoid costume detail disappearing into the cape. Even at this stage, you can change details that you are not happy with. Here, the style of the belt has been slightly altered and Storm's headdress has been added. Now, you have a truly dynamic illustration of Storm.

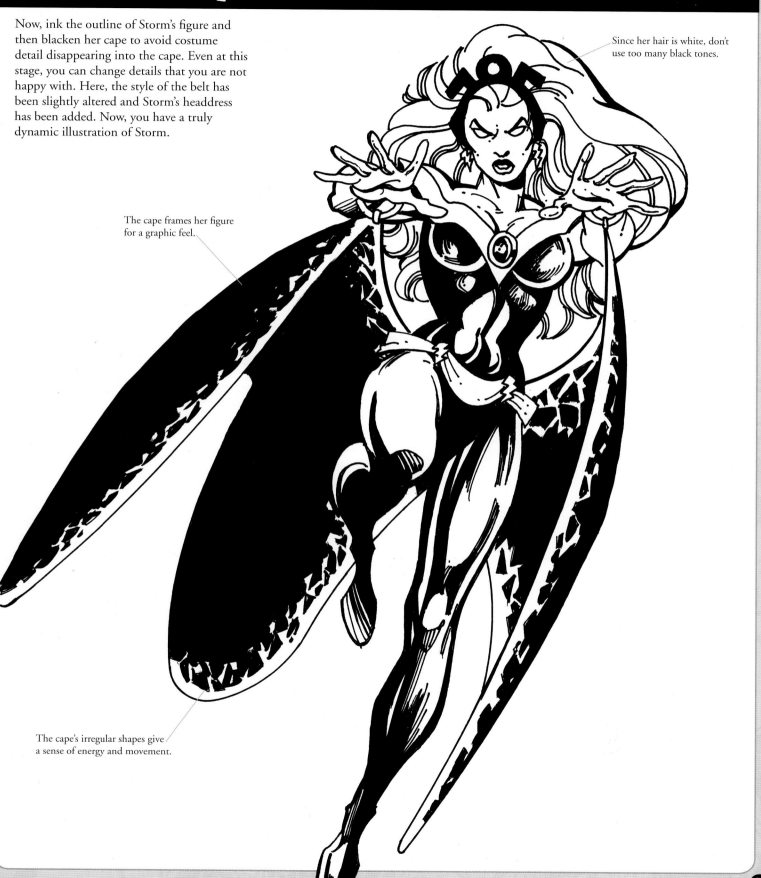

Since her hair is white, don't use too many black tones.

The cape frames her figure for a graphic feel.

The cape's irregular shapes give a sense of energy and movement.

INKING & COLORING

Once you are happy with your pencil drawing, it is time to add ink and color!

Ink used to be added to a comic page because pencil lines were too faint to produce comics from. Now that printing has improved, it is possible for comics to use purely pencil art. However, an inked picture enhances the sense of personality of the penciled art.

Adding color is far more than merely filling in the spaces. Color adds mood to the illustration. A colored picture of Wolverine can look intense, cold, or mean and moody. It all depends on the colors you use.

Over the next few pages you'll learn different inking techniques and effects, how the piece of equipment you choose can affect the style of your work, how to create color moods, and how comic color has changed throughout the ages.

There's lots to learn so let's get started!

EQUIPMENT

INKING

It is rare to see drawings in comics that only use pencils. Comic artists ink their pencil art because inked lines reproduce better in the printed comic. Pens, brushes, or markers can be used to blacken and enhance the lines, giving a finished look.

Dip pens

Dip pens have a removable pen point that you dip in ink to use. The point flexes, which means that you can create different line widths and effects.

Technical pens

Technical pens have a cylinder that you fill with ink. The tips vary in thickness, letting you draw a consistent line.

Dip pen and nibs

Technical pen

Felt-tip pens or markers

There are a wide variety of felt-tips or markers available. These are fine to use to make different marks and effects, but they can create a line that browns or fades with age.

Felt-tip

Fine felt-tip

Wide felt-tip

Biro

Brushes

Brushes are available as fine or thick as you could need and the bristles can be hair or synthetic. However, they all need to be cared for and kept clean. Most artists use a good watercolor brush for inking. Popular sizes to use are two, three, or four.

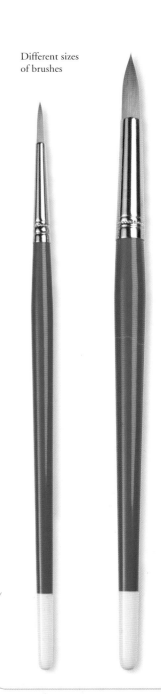

Different sizes of brushes

Ink

As with pencils, you will experiment with many different types of ink. Some artists like the ink to be as black and thick as possible. Try to find an ink that covers well, doesn't clog, and doesn't look "washed out" once it is applied.

Ink for technical pen

Dip pen ink

Correction fluid

Process white

Correction fluid

Correction fluid is white ink that is used to fix those little mistakes all of us make! It is also great to use for special effects, such as turning a black night sky into a star-filled skyscape.

Correction tape

MAKING MARKS

One advantage that brushes and pens have over pencils is that the bristles or nibs flex. This means that you can create special effects, and different types of lines and shading.

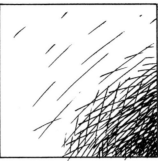

You learned how to crosshatch in the pencil drawing section. This technique can also be effective using a pen.

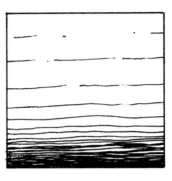

Here, simple, straight lines have been drawn with the gaps between the lines widening. This creates a black to white effect.

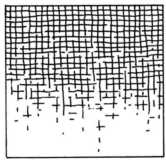

This is a uniform crosshatching effect so there is less build-up of tone. Look at the way the lines fade out at the bottom.

These pen lines, using a thick marker, show how flexible a pen can be. The shape of the stroke makes them almost look like birds.

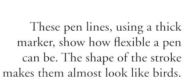

This section was inked and an art knife was dragged through it. This removes ink to create a rain or snow effect.

A block of black tone has been inked using dots. The dots are spaced out until the page is white, creating a good sense of light and shade.

INKING EFFECTS

A MATERIAL WORLD

Inking can make the effects that you have achieved in your pencil drawing even more dramatic. Whether you need to create the look of rough, textured wood, smooth, polished glass, or give your figure outlines, you will find that inking will give your drawings a new depth.

TEXTURES

Rough tree bark can be shown by using a quick brush stroke and alternating between thin and thick lines. Finally, add feathering, which you will learn about on the opposite page.

Smooth lines and expanses of ink and white give this chrome ball a highly polished look.

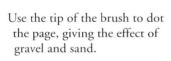

Use the tip of the brush to dot the page, giving the effect of gravel and sand.

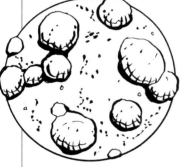

Using the brush's tip, snap your wrist and quickly lift the brush to create natural-looking leaves.

In this picture, smooth liquid, made with flowing lines, is running between the rough bricks, made up of strong lines and dots.

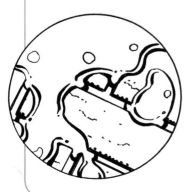

Claws out

In this picture, there are dark areas of black ink on the front of Wolverine's body. This is because the intense fire behind him throws the front of his body into shadow. By inking the shadow before the color is put on, the effect is intense. All these effects reinforce the anger visible on Wolverine's face.

MARVEL EXPERT ADVICE

The best thing that you can do... is play! Try different approaches with a number of different tools—brushes, felt-tips, technical pens—and you'll eventually come up with some tricks of your own that become part of your personal visual style. Some of the things you try may not work, but you'll learn from each attempt until you build up a catalogue of techniques that you will need to call on when you draw figures from the Marvel world.

FEATHERING

Feathering is a term that has nothing to do with feathers! It describes the technique of using short strokes that get thicker as they join the outline. Look at the lines going into the edge of Doc Ock's coat in the picture on the right. This effect builds form and can separate a main object or character from a background or somewhat cluttered scene.

Details of feathering
In this shot, Doc Ock is featured in a split-screen effect. The left side features a feathered inking style that makes him stand out. The right side uses a more graphic, harsh black and white approach. Both looks are effective.

Black vs. white
You also want to make sure your image retains its clarity. In this case, the Silver Surfer has a halo effect around him, created by leaving a small bit of room between the Surfer and the background. This actually makes him pop off the page in a dynamic fashion.

Different approaches
When deciding on a stylistic approach for a piece, decide what you want the shot to communicate. These two shots of Wolverine are similar, but in the one on the left, he is darkened, lit from behind, and details of his costume can be seen. The picture on the right uses a silhouette approach where the figure's outline is completely filled with black ink. It's the same character but with a very different feel.

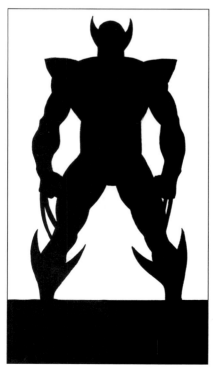

INKING STYLES

PERSONALITY POINTS

If we drew a page of art and gave it to three different inkers, we would get three inked pages back and each would have its own personality. Some inkers use brushes, others use pens, some are precise, others are loose, and some simply have their own style. The inking style adds to the final look.

STEP-BY-STEP

BUILD IT UP
This picture will give you an idea of how a piece evolves as you ink. With each step the shot takes on a different personality.

① **It helps to start with a fully penciled drawing, following the lines as faithfully as possible.**

② **You can alter the weights of the lines with inking tools more easily than with pencil.**

③ **Leave inking the heavy black lines until last. This means that you will avoid smearing the ink.**

FINISHES

Light inking
Some artists use a very light style of inking, as they prefer the color to create more of the impact. In this case we've added enough background detail for the drawing to be considered almost finished once we have erased the pencil lines.

Medium inking
Medium inking builds up the foundations. As you can see, more feathering has been added along with some larger areas of black. This now has a little more depth and weight than before.

Heavy inking
By using heavy inking, the picture as a whole has more weight. We have inked both the background and Thor more heavily than before, which makes the picture have a lot more depth. All three versions are good examples of inking. It all depends what your personal preference is.

EQUIPMENT

COLORFUL CHARACTERS

You have learnt how to draw and ink the illustrations. The only step left is color. Spider-Man may look good in black and white, but he looks absolutely sensational in color. You can use a number of different tools to color your work and we will take a look at each of them.

Chalk

Crayons and chalk

Chalk is useful for blending and covering large areas. It is quite easy to control and blend and so it works for special shading effects. Crayons do not blend as well but, like chalk, they are convenient for covering large areas. You might want to use a different coloring tool for smaller areas.

CRAYONS

Crayon

Felt-tips and markers

Felt tips and markers produce a dense look and come in a variety of colors and sizes. Unlike chalk, a marker's color is consistent and fixed. However, you can buy clear blending markers, which keep the ink wet so that it mixes on the page.

Brushes

B

PILOT

Brushes

Painting with brushes is great for large areas, creating special background effects, or achieving a particular look that dry equipment, such as color pencils, cannot achieve. Brushes are available in a wide range of styles, sizes, and bristle material.

Color markers

Fat marker

Color pencils

Color pencils come in many colors, can be sharpened to a fine point for coloring small areas, and are good to use for shading and blending. They are also easier to use and manipulate than markers.

Color pencils

Paint

There are four basic sorts of paint available. Oils are easy to manipulate, mix, and work with over several days. Acrylics are less flexible and tend to dry faster but they do create a nice, finished look. Watercolors soak or saturate the entire paper you are working on and are not adaptable once they have been applied. Gouache can be thinned like watercolor or applied in a thicker fashion.

Watercolors

Oil

Acrylic

Gouache

MARVEL EXPERT ADVICE

You need to experiment with applying color to find your favorite method. Try all sorts of techniques and tools. A good way to begin is to start with color pencils, which are good to use in order to practice shading and blending. After that you can play around with markers, inks, and paint until you find the method you like best. The paper you use also affects which paint you will choose. For example, watercolors won't work well on a smooth finished Bristol board but will work extremely well on watercolor paper.

DIGITAL COLOR

In recent years it has become typical for comics to have the color applied digitally rather than using paints and markers. Before digital color, blocks of color film called acetate were cut out to match the paint and dye shades on the page. The pages were then printed using this color film. Using digital color means that color can be chosen for every single individual part of the page. The black and white artwork is scanned into a computer and the colorist works in one of several programs to apply the color. More effects are being created all the time, enabling the colorist to create many different looks and textures.

COLOR BASICS

THE PROPERTIES OF COLOR

Color is produced when light strikes an object and is then reflected back to your eyes. Color has three properties. The first is hue, which is a complex term but essentially refers to the color's name. Intensity measures a color's strength and purity. Value describes a color's lightness or darkness.

COLOR WHEEL

A color wheel demonstrates some basic principles of color theory. You can imagine the primary colors—yellow, blue, and red—as the three points of a triangle. Directly in between those hues are the secondary colors, which are mixed from the primary colors. Tertiary colors are made by mixing primary and secondary hues.

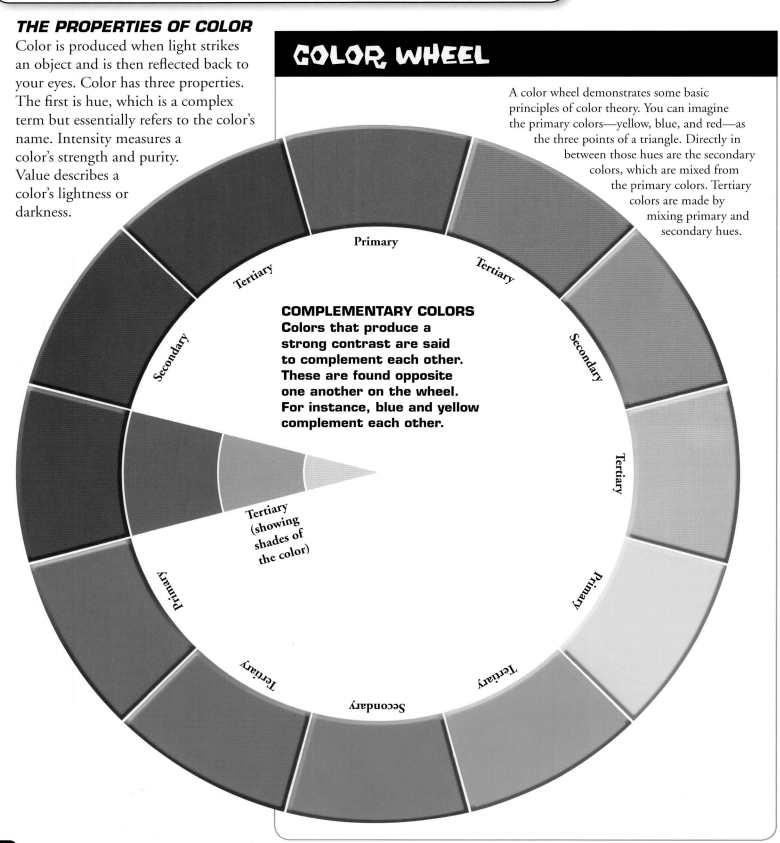

Primary

Tertiary

Tertiary

Secondary

Secondary

COMPLEMENTARY COLORS
Colors that produce a strong contrast are said to complement each other. These are found opposite one another on the wheel. For instance, blue and yellow complement each other.

Tertiary

Tertiary
(showing shades of the color)

Primary

Primary

Tertiary

Tertiary

Secondary

COLOR MOODS

Color affects the mood of an illustration. These three illustrations of Sue Richards use the same line art but create different impressions because each has its own color scheme.

Cold
Blues, purples, and whites tend to be very cold colors. This is helpful if your character is battling arctic conditions!

Hot
Reds, yellows, and oranges create a hot impression, as though Sue is trapped in a heat chamber.

Moody
Dark, flat colors, particularly those that are tertiary colors, give a very moody feel to the illustration.

Fire and ice
Using different environments offers a chance to show how color can affect your story. A story with Thor summoning fire (left) will feature hot reds, yellows, and oranges. A story featuring Iceman (below) will use cold blues, purples, and whites.

COMIC COLOR

GOLDEN AGE COLOR

For 50 years, comic coloring was limited. A black and white copy of the art would be colored using inks and dyes. Each color was given a code, such as R2B3, describing the mixture of red and blue. The range of colors used was not vast.

Old vs. new

The picture of Spider-Man below shows the way color used to be applied. The effect is flat. The other picture of Spidey shows how colorists can now use various colors, mixes, and effects to layer their work.

Paint

One comic coloring technique that has grown popular is to produce a story with paint. The artist paints each scene for a stunning finished product.

1) The artist, Brandon Peterson, did a pencil layout to send to the book designer.

2) Once the layout was approved, he fleshed out the figures and penciled in details.

3) He then inked the drawing, using black tones to make the picture more dramatic.

4) Finally, Brandon scanned the picture into his computer and colored it digitally for a detailed, dynamic illustration.

COVER ART
Take a look at the artwork on the cover of this book. Brandon Peterson did not simply create the picture in one stage.
He received a brief from the book's designer, describing what the picture should show. Then he used all the stages that you have learnt about to create this exciting picture of Spider-Man and the Green Goblin.

WOLVERINE

A member of the mutant team called the X-Men, Wolverine may be small but he is incredibly powerful. His main weapons are his retractable claws, which spring from his forearms. He is a ferocious combatant in battle, as shown by his gritted-fang grimace. His muscular legs and crouching, wolf-like stance enable him to pounce on his enemies, slashing them with his pointed talons. You'll need to use your skills in drawing humans and monsters to capture this mutant!

GIANT-SIZE X-MEN

In May 1975, the "new" X-Men debuted in a double-sized issue. This illustration shows the mutants bursting through the cover. (Cover art by Gil Kane)

CHARACTER HISTORY

Witnessing the murder of his father brought young James Howlett's latent mutant abilities to the surface. Renamed Logan, he began to prefer the company of wild animals to that of humans, spending time with a pack of wolves and taking the name "Wolverine." A group of Weapon X scientists, who turn beings into living weapons, bonded molecules of an iron alloy called adamantium to his claws, making them virtually unbreakable. They also inserted

memory implants in his brain, so that Wolverine has trouble remembering his true past. Some time later, Logan joined the X-Men at Professor Xavier's request and the group is the closest thing he has to family. Wolverine now has a cause to fight for: to battle those who threaten humanity.

WOLVERINE IN ACTION

This picture shows Wolverine's key features: his claws, his super-strong muscles, and his stance as he prepares to attack.

MARVEL EXPERT ADVICE

Like Spider-Man and Storm, Wolverine has a unique build. Whereas Storm is quite tall and Spider-Man is thin and quirky, Wolverine is a short, solid figure. As fun and happy-go-lucky as Spider-Man might be, Wolverine is a generally gloomy, unhappy sort of guy. His arms and legs should be incredibly thick and almost look out of proportion with the rest of him. He should also look like he could rip a tank apart with his claws.

ROUGH PENCIL DRAWING

This illustration of Wolverine draws attention to his claws and gives the outline of his mask. It shows that you don't always have to have a full figure shot. This tight shot showing him from the waist up closes in on the features that are typically Wolverine: his muscles, strong upper body, and his claws!

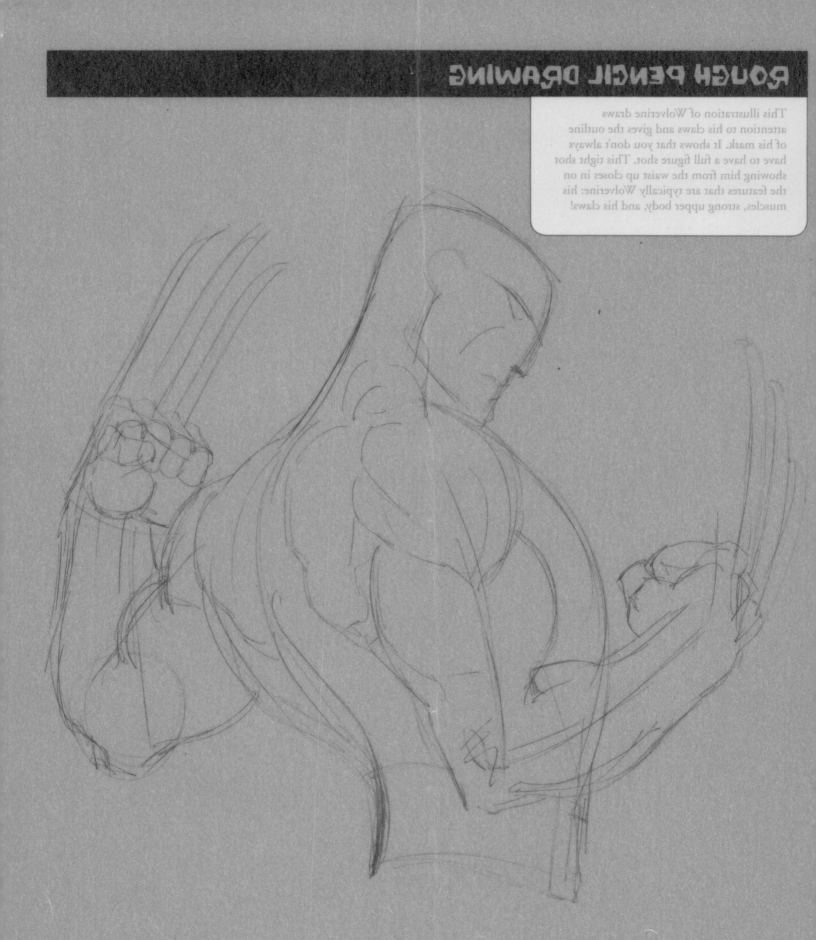

This illustration of Wolverine draws attention to his claws and gives the outline of his mask. It shows that you don't always have to have a full figure shot. This tight shot showing him from the waist up closes in on the features that are typically Wolverine: his muscles, strong upper body, and his claws!

FINAL PENCIL DRAWING

Next, add the shading. If you imagine a light source on the right side of the picture, the left side will be in shadow. At this stage, you can fill in Wolverine's mask and stress the thickness of his arms. Even if this figure was in silhouette, you could tell who he was.

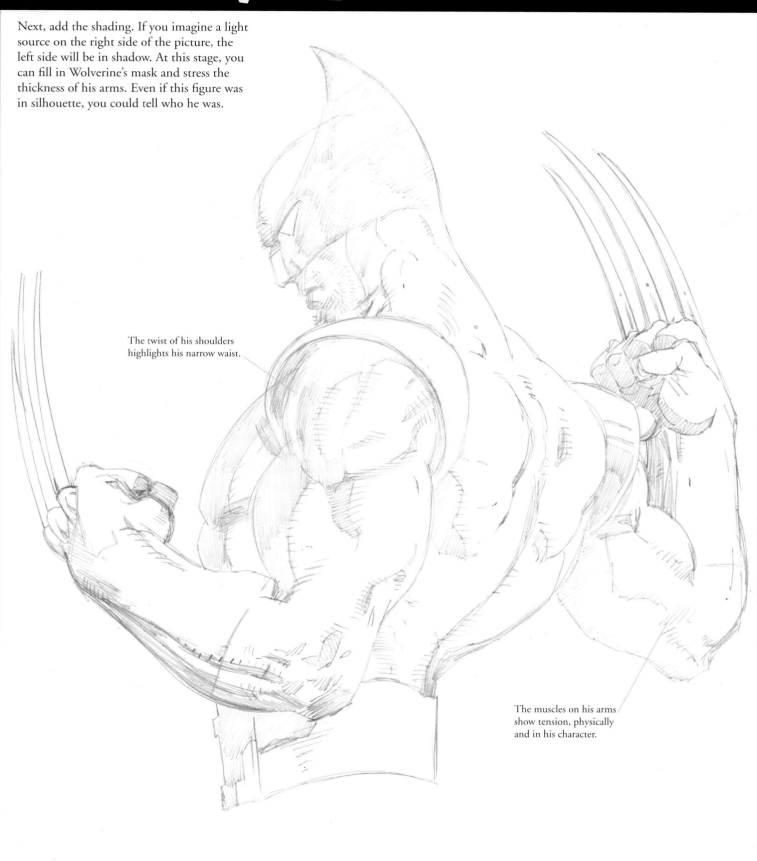

The twist of his shoulders highlights his narrow waist.

The muscles on his arms show tension, physically and in his character.

IDENTIFYING DETAILS

Wolverine's key visual features are his large muscles, his wolf-like hairstyle, and, of course, his retractable claws. It is important to convey the strength of his claws and the gleaming adamantium that they're made of. The use of gray and white ink on the blades creates a metallic effect. With claws out and a determined look on his face, Wolverine is ready to rip his enemies to shreds!

THE FACE

Here you can see Wolverine's complete face. His wild hair resembles a wolf's and his mouth is set into a snarl. He clenches his teeth, mustering all his strength to attack his enemy. Look at photographs of wolves attacking and you'll see the similarities with Wolverine. You can also see his massive tendons and muscles that stand out strongly, emphasizing his strength.

His gritted teeth reinforce his strong-jawed look.

THE BODY

Wolverine more than makes up for his short stature with his huge muscle power. His upper body is incredibly strong, allowing him to use his claws to great effect. His leg muscles are also amazingly powerful. They need to be as he crouches and pounces on unsuspecting foes. Another animal-like feature of his body is the thick hair on his arms. These examples reveal that the character of figures can be shown through the body as well as the face.

His muscles can be seen through his costume.

FINAL INKED DRAWING

Use a nibbed pen and brush to ink
Wolverine. A technical pen and French curve
are perfect for the claws. For the hair on the
arms, use a very fine nib and a light touch.
The curve of the mask matches the curve
of his claws and they work well together.
Congratulations—you've managed to
capture this marvellous mutant.

Bring the claws to a
sharp point.

The shading on the
shoulder pieces make
them look reflective.

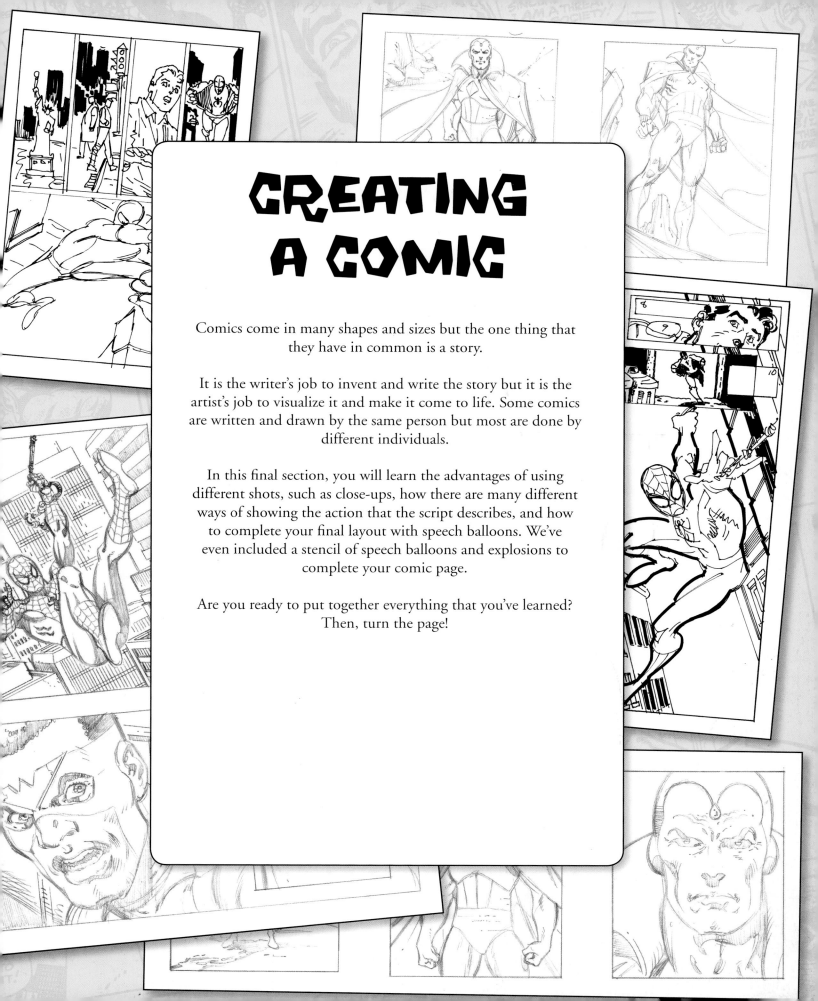

CREATING A COMIC

Comics come in many shapes and sizes but the one thing that they have in common is a story.

It is the writer's job to invent and write the story but it is the artist's job to visualize it and make it come to life. Some comics are written and drawn by the same person but most are done by different individuals.

In this final section, you will learn the advantages of using different shots, such as close-ups, how there are many different ways of showing the action that the script describes, and how to complete your final layout with speech balloons. We've even included a stencil of speech balloons and explosions to complete your comic page.

Are you ready to put together everything that you've learned? Then, turn the page!

SHOTS & ANGLES

THE RIGHT ANGLE

Every comic book either starts with a plot, which describes the story's flow and direction, or a full script, which breaks the story down to each comic page and panel, and includes all the dialogue for the characters. The artist uses both of these as a guide to work from. Comic scripts also use a unique language or terminology to indicate the type of shots or angles that are required. It is useful for artists to think of themselves as a camera, moving in and out and sweeping or panning across a particular scene. Think of how you might position yourself to see a particular bit of action and that is the angle you will want to draw it from.

ESTABLISHING SHOT
This is a long shot from far away. It is a wide view of the entire scene, showing the background details and the position of the Vision. The emphasis in this shot is on the scene itself.

MEDIUM SHOT
In this shot, the camera moves in closer. A bit of the background is still visible while the figure is cropped. The main character is emphasized. It is in between an establishing shot and a close-up.

CLOSE-UP
This shot is achieved by the camera moving in even tighter toward the figure. Here the close-up focuses on the Vision's face and the emphasis is on the emotion displayed on his face.

Establishing shot

Medium shot

Close-up

Up shot

In the shot on the far left, the camera is low on the ground, looking up toward the Vision. This makes him take on a position of power. The tall rock formations in the background add to this sense of height.

Down shot

In the shot on the left, the camera seems to be several feet off the ground. It places the reader above the Vision and implies that he is looking up at something of interest.

Composition

If the writer asks for a shot of Spider-Man swinging through the city, you want to frame Spidey and the background properly. Place the whole figure in the panel with room between him and the edges. Which is right out of these two versions?

Inset panel

An inset panel is a good way to show two shots in one main panel. In the drawing below, we see what the Falcon is looking at without having to jump between panels.

THE SCRIPT

TAKE ONE!

The script gives descriptions of each panel and the dialogue and captions. Here, the writer has used five panels to show Peter Parker react to a scream and change into Spider-Man.

The Amazing Spider-Man #XXX
Script for 22 pages
Joe Writer (444) 555-0000

Panel One
LONG SHOT. Night. New York City, focusing on Manhattan.

1 CAP: New York City.
2 CAP: Home of dirt, grime, rampant crime, enough trash to bury a country--
3 CAP: --and a tax rate that'll strangle you.
4 CAP: But it's HOME.

Panel Two
MEDIUM SHOT. Peter Parker walking along a quiet sidewalk.
5 CAP: And you gotta love it.
6 CAP: Not that I wouldn't mind learning to love a sandy beach in Hawaii.
7 OFF: AIIEEE!

Panel Three
Close on Peter as he reacts with alarm to scream off panel.
8 CAP: Anywhere quiet. Where nothing goes wrong.
9 OFF: HELLLP MEEE!

Panel Four
Peter ducks into a deserted alley pulling open his jacket and shirt to reveal his Spider-Man costume. Heavy shadows with single, dim light.

10 CAP: But when something does go wrong--

Panel Five
Dramatic shot of Spider-Man swinging up out of the alley, ready for action.
11 SPIDEY: --the amazing, spectacular, incredibly scintillating SPIDER-MAN is ready to rock!
12 SPIDEY: If I wasn't, I'd be in violation of page three, paragraph two of my official Super Hero contract!
13 SPIDEY: Which is right after the paragraph that tells us not to talk to ourselves!

Comments

It's the artist's job to mold the script into a visually interesting scene. Read the script and look at the comments below to see how you could represent this story.

• The captions (CAP) represent Peter Parker's thoughts.
• His thoughts tell us that he is in New York, so pick a visual to show it, like the Statue of Liberty.
• The scream comes from off panel (OFF), which means that we don't know who is screaming.
• Emphasize the page's most important scene. In this case, it's the appearance of Spider-Man!

THUMBNAILS

Thumbnails are the quick, small sketches that show how the artist thinks a particular scene, panel, or page will look. When working on a page, the artists sketch thumbnails so they can play around with page layout, camera angles, and composition. Visualizing your ideas like this means that you can decide which style you like best.

Layout 1

The long thin panels give the page a strong vertical feel. They illustrate the height of New York's buildings and emphasize Spider-Man leaping up out of the alley.

Layout 2

This is a more basic approach, starting with a wide scene shot and then moving down to the street. It seems a bit more anonymous than the first layout.

Layout 3

This page has a sense of rhythm as each of the top panels has been drawn the same size. It may not be as visually interesting as the first layout but it is effective in its own way.

FINAL LAYOUT

FINAL STRETCH

Out of the thumbnail layouts on the previous page, we have chosen to use the first one. We have made some minor alterations. In this larger marker layout (right), we have changed Spider-Man's figure because it looked like he was standing on his head! We have also placed the captions and word balloons.

Marker layout

In the fifth panel of this marker layout, the picture of Spider-Man is more effective because it has greater depth and it is clear that he has leapt out of the alley. We have used foreshortening on his left hand, making the pose more dynamic than in the original.

HOPELESSLY *GROUNDED* IN THE STAGNANT, BRINE-FILLED POOL, THE HULK WRITHED IN *LITTER* AGONY AS IRON MAN SENT A HIGH-VOLTAGE ELECTRIC *CHARGE* CRACKLING FROM HIS TRANSISTORIZED GAUNTLETS

WORDS AND SOUNDS

Word balloons are an important part of page and character design. Many Marvel heroes and villains have sounds that are unique to them. For example, "thwipt" is the sound of Spider-Man shooting a webline and "snikt" is the sound of Wolverine popping his claws. "Sptanng" might be the sound of a bullet bouncing off Captain America's shield. In this illustration, the angular, rough shape of the speech balloon with large, red letters for the scream gives the reader the feeling that the Hulk is in a great deal of pain. You can use the stencil at the back of this book to add speech balloons to your layout.

3) The inking stage gives the art a more graphic feel. Use the inking techniques that you have learnt to add texture to the buildings and shading to Spider-Man.

PUT IT TOGETHER
This pencil drawing shows what the page looks like before inking. It is certainly different from the original thumbnails, as you can tell by looking at the grid for the buildings in panel one. Put as much detail as possible into your pencil drawing so that it is easier to move on to inking.

1) Use the marker layout as a guide. If you have a light-table, put your page over the marker layout so that you can keep the correct layout and proportions.

2) Tighten up the buildings in panel one and make sure that the perspective is correct in panel five.

STEP-BY-STEP

THE END!

I still remember the first time I ever saw a comic book. I was seven-years-old, playing hide-and-seek with some of the kids in the neighborhood and I saw a kid reading a comic. Just one look through his stack of copies and I was quickly hooked on the striking characters and the fantastic scenes that leapt off the page at me!

Every comic-lover has their own story of how they first got into comics and how they wished they could draw the figures that they saw on the page.

When you first opened this book, you may not have been able to draw anything more than a basic stick figure. Now, your sketchbook features Spider-Man swinging through New York City and the Fantastic Four saving the day.

Using this book, you have learnt how to draw figures, make your characters pack a punch, add personality to your drawing by inking, and create a colorful comic page.

You've made a great start but it's just the beginning.

So, remember—keep drawing and, most of all, enjoy it!

Comics

• Your first source of inspiration will always be the Marvel comics themselves. Read the works of the present, as well as the classics of the past, to see what the earlier artists created and what's being done now.

• You will probably find that there are certain artists that you really like. Now that you have studied the techniques of drawing, you will have a better understanding of how your favorite artists achieve their effects and will be able to copy some of them yourself.

Books

• Go to the art departments of your local library or bookstore and you will find many books on different aspects of drawing that will help you expand your knowledge.

• Books on Marvel characters are also useful. The more you understand about the personality of a character, the better your drawings will be. These books will also show you different drawing styles from the Golden Age of comics to the present day. Dorling Kindersley publish *The Avengers – The Ultimate Guide, Fantastic Four – The Ultimate Guide, Spider-Man – The Ultimate Guide,* and *X-Men – The Ultimate Guide.*

Website

• www.marvel.com is the official Marvel website where you can get up-to-date information on new comics as well as profiles on characters and groups.

• www.marveldirectory.com is another website with character profiles. It also features good simple poses of characters for you to use as reference.

Other

• Posable action figures that you may have are useful for getting the details and proportions of figures correct.

• If you have access to a computer, you can find images and basic line drawings in wordprocessing packages. You can use this "clip art" as reference material for figures and objects.

INDEX

ACKNOWLEDGMENTS

AUTHOR ACKNOWLEDGMENTS

Anyone working in this industry has to acknowledge the genius of those who created a rich tapestry of characters that exist to this day. Jerry Siegel and Joe Shuster, Bob Kane, Bill Finger, Gardner Fox, Gil Kane, Stan Lee, Jack Kirby, Curt Swan, Neal Adams, and a host of others, too numerous to mention, dreamed up stories and characters that will endure forever. Thanks as well to all the artists whose work graced these pages.

On a more personal note, a tip of the hat to Walter Simonson for his encouragement so long ago, to Mike Grell for opening doors, and Dick Giordano, Gerry Conway, and Mike Carlin for letting me run.

And thanks to my parents, John and Joan, for building that first drawing table and supporting the pursuit of a dream.

Dan Jurgens

September, 2005

PUBLISHER'S ACKNOWLEDGMENTS

DORLING KINDERSLEY would like to thank Matthew Primack and James Hinton at Marvel UK, Neil Kelly for editorial assistance, Jon Hall for the color wheel and design assistance, and Mika Kean-Hammerson for design assistance. DK would also like to thank Brandon Peterson for the front cover art.